Derwin Gray gives readers a fresh word on prayer. He illuminates, illustrates, and communicates the hope we all need to find strength in divine communion. There is much we can do after we pray. There is nothing we should do before we pray. Pastor Gray's words will help you bend your knees and then stand in faith.

Max Lucado, pastor and author

Everyone at one point in their lives finds themselves asking big questions about God. One of them being, "Do my prayers matter?", and thankfully we have a resource from Dr. Gray helping us see the ways our prayers change us, connect us to God, and lead us to worship Him.

Jamie Ivey, bestselling author and
host of *The Happy Hour with Jamie Ivey* podcast

This is the book on the power of prayer that this generation needs. In these eye-opening pages, my friend Derwin Gray graciously reveals what God's Word actually says about the life that's available to us when we live a life of prayer. *God, Do You Hear Me?* will reignite a fire within you to know God for real, and to experience the full life he has for you. These words will transform how you see God, how you talk to God, and how you live.

Hosanna Wong, international speaker, spoken word
artist, and author of *How (Not) to Save the World*

It's impossible to grow in the spiritual life without a commitment to prayer. Yet, where do we begin? This was the question Jesus' first disciples asked, and it gets repeated in every generation. This is why I'm so thankful for Derwin Gray and this book. With winsome storytelling, fresh perspectives, and rich theology, Derwin guides us through the most important prayer Jesus taught us. I'll be recommending this to many!

Rich Villodas, lead pastor of New Life Fellowship
and author of *The Deeply Formed Life*

Simply put, Dr. Derwin Gray has done it again. His words have taken me on a theological journey that has reminded me of who my Father is and who I am to my Father. Do your soul a favor, read this book.

Albert Tate, lead pastor of Fellowship Church

DR. DERWIN L. GRAY

Bestselling author of *The Good Life*

God,
do you
hear
me?

Discover the prayer God always answers

Foreword by Lysa TerKeurst

B&H
PUBLISHING
NASHVILLE, TENNESSEE

Published by B&H Publishing Group
Nashville, Tennessee

Dewey Decimal: 226.96
Subject Heading: PRAYER / LORD'S PRAYER / JESUS
CHRIST—PRAYERS

Unless otherwise noted, all Scripture quotations are taken from the Christian Standard Bible®, Copyright © 2017 by Holman Bible Publishers. Used by permission. Christian Standard Bible® and CSB® are federally registered trademarks of Holman Bible Publishers.

Also used: New Living Translation (NLT), copyright © 1996, 2004, 2015 by Tyndale House Foundation. Used by permission of Tyndale House Publishers, Inc., Carol Stream, Illinois 60188. All rights reserved.

Also used: New International Version®, NIV® (NIV), copyright ©1973, 1978, 1984, 2011 by Biblica, Inc.® Used by permission. All rights reserved worldwide.

Cover design by A. Micah Smith.
Author photo © Transformation Church.

Published in association with The Bindery Agency,
www.TheBinderyAgency.com.

It is the Publisher's goal to minimize disruption caused by technical errors or invalid websites. While all links are active at the time of publication, because of the dynamic nature of the internet, some web addresses or links contained in this book may have changed and may no longer be valid. B&H Publishing Group bears no responsibility for the continuity or content of the external site, nor for that of subsequent links. Contact the external site for answers to questions regarding its content.

1 2 3 4 5 6 7 • 26 25 24 23 22 21

To Vicki:
I dedicate *God, Do You Hear Me?* to you.
You are the love of my life,
my best friend.
You have inspired me in more ways than I can count.
Your love for Jesus and our children makes me want
to be a better man.
You serve Transformation Church with deep gospel convictions
and an elegance in leadership that is infectious and powerful.

Acknowledgments

Writing a book is a team sport. I have a fabulous team. Chris, Alex, and Kristel, thank you. Your contributions are priceless, your friendship is invaluable, and your support is immeasurable. Bravo Team PD! Well done!

Presley and Jeremiah, thanks for believing in your dad. Your support and encouragement mean the world to me. You inspire me to be the best I can be.

To the B&H team, thank you. You make writing books fun! And thank you for believing in me as an author.

I want to thank my agent, Alexander Field, for his encouragement and support.

And finally, to the Transformation Church Family, thank you! As I pray for you, as I serve you, God the Holy Spirit is growing me as a disciple of King Jesus. May *God, Do You Hear Me?* teach us to pray.

Contents

Foreword

There's something different about a person who prays. I mean, a person who really prays. My friend Derwin is this kind of person. I'm not sure I've ever met someone more committed to bringing everything back to Jesus. The way he thinks is a direct reflection of the way he prays. The way he speaks is a reflection of the way he prays. And the way he doesn't seem to freak out about things is a reflection of the way he prays.

And what makes those around him want to lean in to his wisdom on prayer is that he's not annoying about the effectiveness of his prayer life. He owns it. But he doesn't flaunt it. He is settled and secure without being condescending or cocky.

But I think the most important thing you should know is that his life isn't void of truly crappy and chaotic hardships. He's like me. He's like you. His life gets hard sometimes. It doesn't all tie up in a nice, neat bow. He gets hurt, confused, and caught off guard. He is sometimes overlooked and underappreciated. He has questions, unresolved issues, and things he wishes were different about both his private world and the world at large. And that's why he's so very qualified to write a book to help the rest of us confidently pray while constantly wrestling through stuff.

He is highly educated in theology but also acutely aware of the realities of humanity.

That's precisely the reason I can trust the words penned on these pages. I can't handle being preached at about how I need to do better in my prayer life. I already know that. And honestly, I feel kind of blah and want to roll my eyes when people with much more tidy lives than mine try to attribute my hardships to something I'm lacking in my prayer life. Nothing like having a little salt poured into a gaping wound, right?!

Derwin's life doesn't smell as stuffy as a library or as sterile as a laboratory. Its aroma is authenticity with a healthy splash of hardship.

This is what I need in a book on prayer. It's not that I need my prayers to be longer or more official sounding or more consistent. And it's definitely not that my prayers need to be organized or impressive. No, they need to be more connected to the heart of Jesus. The compassion of Jesus. The gentle grace and unwavering truth of Jesus. The strength and stamina of Jesus. And the reality of Jesus.

I often stress about my issues. Fret about my fears. Talk about my turmoil. Process my problems. Seek help and wisdom and counsel from smart people. And all of that can be healthy and good.

But, have I really prayed about it all? Too many times I've only thought about it and stressed over it. And therein lies the problem. I'm missing out on tapping into the power of the One who knows all, carries all, and covers all with a peace that passes understanding. Those other activities can be a resource but they can't ever be "the source" from where my real help comes.

I think the only regret you'll have in diving into this book is that you didn't have it sooner. But for such a time as this, let's together open it now and prepare to be understood and overwhelmed by what's really possible with prayer.

Lysa TerKeurst

CHAPTER 1

Sandcastles

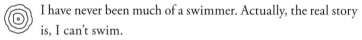 I have never been much of a swimmer. Actually, the real story is, I can't swim.

Once on vacation in Grenada, I was splashing around in the beautiful turquoise water, attempting to swim. I suspect my attempt must have looked like a comedy routine because some local boys said to me in an epic accent, "Look at you, man! You can't even swim with all those big muscles!" I looked at them and said in what I was hoping to be a Grenadian accent, "No man! I can't swim! I never learned how!" Even now, all these years later, it brings a smile to my face.

I am not really a beach or ocean kind of guy either, but my wife and children love being on the sand. My daughter, Presley, loves it so much that she chose to go to the University of North Carolina at Wilmington, a beach community not too far from Oak Island. Oak Island is a place my daughter and I treasure. It is our own Narnia, a mystical, mysterious meeting place where our hearts bonded. From ages seven to eighteen, Presley would accompany me as my "wing-woman" to Oak Island where I would preach at a summer youth camp. I watched her grow from an elementary student, through the awkward middle school years, into a beautiful senior in high school, on these weeklong summer adventures. We made so many beautiful memories over the years, from chasing each other through the old military forts to eating sushi every night for dinner, and having lunch at Provisions, where we would order the famous "1 Pound Shrimp Special."

God uses places and spaces to connect us to his heart and to each other. The beach is one of those places for the House of Gray. My family loves the beach and ocean, but, me, not so much. It's not where I would choose to go by myself, but out of love for my people and the smiles it brings to their faces, I go and go often.

Here is my beach routine: I marinate on the beach, chillaxing in a beach chair under a canopy that blocks the sun. Then I cover myself with a large beach towel that blocks the sunrays that escaped the canopy. I get my Bible, a good theology book, a cold, fruity drink, and I enjoy myself in the shade.

Why, you ask? First, as I already said, I can't swim. Second, there are creatures in the ocean that can eat me. In my mind, I believe a tiger shark would find me appealing to eat. At 5'11", 260 pounds of pure dark muscularity, I'd be like a gourmet meal. No thanks! Derwin is not getting in the water. Third, the Lord has blessed me with an incredible tan, so there is no need for me to cook myself like a rotisserie chicken in the sun.

Rising Tides, Roaring Wind, and Crashing Waves

Do you ever watch kids build sandcastles on the beach? When I'm sitting under my umbrella, I enjoy watching them, because they are so patient and meticulous about building something that they know will be soon wiped away by the rising tide and crashing waves. As I marinate on this thought, it reminds me that we do the same thing with our lives. We fervently work with meticulous skill, intentionally trying to build *The Good Life*,[1] which typically means amassing wealth, power, and status through our jobs. Often, we find ourselves racked with anxiety, exhaustion, bitterness, and frustration because the sandcastles we have worked so hard to build are wiped away by the rising tides and cruel waves that crash on our lives.

WE FIND OURSELVES RACKED WITH ANXIETY, EXHAUSTION, BITTERNESS, AND FRUSTRATION BECAUSE THE SANDCASTLES WE HAVE WORKED SO HARD TO BUILD ARE WIPED AWAY BY THE RISING TIDES AND CRUEL WAVES THAT CRASH ON OUR LIVES.

Two thousand years ago, a poor traveling Jewish preacher from the trailer park town of Nazareth dropped some timeless wisdom on humanity about just this topic. It's timely for you and me:

> "Therefore, everyone who hears these words of mine and acts on them will be like a wise man who built his house on the rock. The rain fell, the rivers rose, and the winds blew and pounded that house. Yet it didn't collapse, because its foundation was on the rock. But everyone who hears these words of mine and doesn't act on them will be like a foolish man who built his house on the sand. The rain fell, the rivers rose, the winds blew

---

[1] See my book, *The Good Life: What Jesus Teaches about Finding True Happiness* (Nashville, B&H Publishing, 2020).

and pounded that house, and it collapsed. It collapsed with a great crash."

When Jesus had finished saying these things, the crowds were astonished at his teaching, because he was teaching them like one who had authority, and not like their scribes. (Matt. 7:24–29)

If we will allow the Spirit of God to speak afresh to us, his life-giving words can transform us. We, too, can be "astonished" at Jesus' teaching. When we build our lives on sand, we will not have the ability to overcome the rising tides and crashing waves. Jesus wants to give us a collapse-proof life.

Paul, one of Jesus' earliest and most loyal Jewish followers, wrote these hope-intoxicated words:

No, in all these things we are more than conquerors through him who loved us. For I am persuaded that neither death nor life, nor angels nor rulers, nor things present nor things to come, nor powers, nor height nor depth, nor any other created thing will be able to separate us from the love of God that is in Christ Jesus our Lord. (Rom. 8:37–39)

Hypernikōmen

The word *conqueror* in Greek is *hypernikōmen*. It means to "keep on winning a glorious victory."[2] Jesus resoundingly won the battle against humanity's great enemy, the dark powers of sin and

---

[2] J. A. Witmer, *Romans*, in J. F. Walvoord and R. B. Zuck (eds.), *The Bible Knowledge Commentary: An Exposition of the Scriptures*, vol. 2 (Wheaton, IL: Victor Books, 1985), 475.

death. Sin and death are invasive species that do not belong in God's good creation. Messiah Jesus triumphed over and disarmed these dark powers with his death and resurrection.

> But thank God! He gives us victory over sin and death through our Lord Jesus Christ. (1 Cor. 15:57 NLT)

> You were dead because of your sins and because your sinful nature was not yet cut away. Then God made you alive with Christ, for he forgave all our sins. He canceled the record of the charges against us and took it away by nailing it to the cross. In this way, he disarmed the spiritual rulers and authorities. He shamed them publicly by his victory over them on the cross. (Col. 2:13–15 NLT)

The One who is "grace upon grace" fights our battles (John 1:16). His weapon of victory was his sinless life, his sacrificial atoning death on the cross, his glorious resurrection, his sending of the Spirit, and his future glorious return. King Jesus' victorious life, which we participate in, makes us overcomers. We are strengthened by the sound of the stone being rolled away from his tomb. Jesus' tomb is empty, and because his tomb is empty, we can be filled by the "Spirit of Jesus Christ" himself (Phil. 1:19; Gal. 5:22–24). The One who walked out of the tomb now wants to walk into our lives and live in and through us. We are coheirs of a kingdom that is unshakable, irreplaceable, and eternally durable. When the rising tides and crashing waves come:

> We may be afflicted, but in Christ, we are not crushed.

We may be perplexed, but in Jesus, we will not lose hope.

We may be persecuted, but in Immanuel, the God who is with us, we will never be abandoned.

We may be struck down, but in Christ Jesus, the King of kings, we will never be destroyed.

What the enemy means for evil, Jesus transforms for our good.

Our lives in Christ are not built on a temporary foundation like sand. In Jesus, our lives are built on the Eternal Rock: "He alone is my rock and my salvation, my stronghold; I will never be shaken" (Ps. 62:2). We can never be shaken loose from the grip of his grace. In Christ, we are not a sandcastle-kind-of-people because Jesus is our firm foundation.

2020 Was Like an Episode of *The Twilight Zone*

I cannot remember the first time I watched an episode of *The Twilight Zone*, but I have been a fan of the TV show for years. I resonate with it because its creator, Rod Serling, took science fiction, cultural issues, suspense, horror, and psychology and created a show that was thought-provoking. The year 2020 was like an episode of *The Twilight Zone*, and each of us had a starring role.

In 2020, the rising tides, accompanied by hurricane-force winds, earthquakes, and a tsunami-sized wave crashed against humanity. The events of the year revealed that our lives are built on sand.

The novel coronavirus, which leads to the COVID-19 disease, descended on us. People got sick. Loved ones died. Unemployment skyrocketed. The American economy, along with the world's economy, raced toward recession.[3] Uncertainty became a blinding fog. Anxiety was around every corner. Some people were not sure where their next meal was coming from. At Transformation Church,[4] where I serve as cofounder and lead elder pastor, we fed more than four hundred families per week who had been impacted by the recession. We started Transformation Church during a recession and found ourselves in another one.

In addition to these economic waves, many white Americans also awoke to issues of systemic racism and racial injustice that have haunted our country since her inception after several high-profile incidents, like the killing of George Floyd, shook us from our slumber. The Band-Aid that has unsuccessfully covered up the racial trauma in America was removed, exposing the unhealed wound for what it is. We clearly saw that as Americans we stand divided, unsure of what tomorrow may bring. The borders that divide Americans are growing wider by the day.

---

[3] Scott Horsley, "It's Official: U.S. Economy Is in a Recession," NPR, June 8, 2020, https://www.npr.org/sections/coronavirus-live-updates/2020/06/08/872336272/its-official-scorekeepers-say-u-s-economy-is-in-a-recession (accessed June 30, 2020).

[4] To learn more about Transformation Church, go to transformationchurch.tc.

I Do What I Do Not Want to Do

As we have realized the world around us is in desperate need of redemption, our behavior reminds us that the interior part of our lives is also in need of redemption. What is in us is, by far, worse than what is outside of us. Jesus said, "For from within, out of people's hearts, come evil thoughts, sexual immoralities, thefts, murders, adulteries, greed, evil actions, deceit, self-indulgence, envy, slander, pride, and foolishness. All these evil things come from within and defile a person" (Mark 7:21–23). No wonder the apostle Paul said, "For I do not understand what I am doing, because I do not practice what I want to do, but I do what I hate" (Rom. 7:15).

We do not love our neighbors as we are called to love.

We do not forgive people as we are called to forgive.

We do not serve people as we are called to serve.

We do not give generously as we are called to give.

Instead, we live in the prison of our past hurts, thus hurting people in the present. We are tormented by addictions. We are the problem that plagues our world.

What hope is there for us?

As you will discover throughout this book, we have a deliverer, a redeemer, a sin-defeater, a death-killer, who out of a heart of endless love, gave his life *for* us, to give his life *to* us, so he can live his overcoming life *through* us! With Paul, we cry out, "Thanks be to God, who delivers me through Jesus Christ our Lord!" (Rom. 7:25 NIV).

Building Our Lives on the Rock

Life is hard. There is so much to overcome. Many of us, perhaps instinctively, turn to God in these moments. We cry out in prayer.

And in the crucible when we are pressed from side-to-side and top-to-bottom, we ask,

> "God, when I pray, do you hear me?"

> "Jesus, are my prayers hitting the ceiling and crashing back to the floor?"

> "Father, am I praying wrong?"

> "I would pray more if I knew how to pray."

> "Are my prayers just empty words going into empty space?"

> "Is anybody even there . . . ?"

Through the pages of this book, I am going to hold your hand and journey with you, not as an expert, but as a fellow traveler, in learning and living the prayer that God always answers.

The prayer that God always answers is what is commonly called the Lord's Prayer (Matt. 6:9–13). The Lord's Prayer is the firm foundation that God builds our lives on the Rock.

Prayer is the secret place where we find God waiting for us.

Prayer is the door we enter to discover God's heart of unending grace.

Prayer is the home we have always wanted, where we can crawl into our Father's lap.

Prayer is a priceless gift. Sadly, many of us rarely spend time enjoying the gift. Thus, we miss enjoying Jesus.

In the fourth century, St. Augustine, the renowned North African pastor, wrote, "True, whole prayer is nothing but love."[5] Jesus longs to teach us how to pray so we can be lost in his love. Nearly a thousand years later, Julian of Norwich, prayed,

> For we are so preciously loved by God that we cannot even comprehend it. No Created being can ever know how much and how sweetly and tenderly God loves them. It is only with the help of his grace that we're able to persevere in spiritual contemplation with endless wonder at his high, surpassing, immeasurable love which our Lord in his goodness has for us.[6]

Prayer is more than just talking to God. Nineteenth-century Danish philosopher, Søren Kierkegaard wrote, "A man prayed, and at first he thought that prayer was talking. But he became more and more quiet until in the end he realized that prayer was listening."[7] The more we immerse ourselves in the sacred Scriptures—the Bible—the better our ears attune to the voice of God, who speaks love over us.

Prayer is more than just asking God for stuff. Jesus said, God "already knows what we need" (Matt. 6:25–32). So, what then is prayer? Prayer is a holy longing to be with God, to experience his love that surpasses understanding, to be embraced by his merciful

---

[5] Richard Foster and James Bryan Smith, *Devotional Classics* (San Francisco: Harper One, 1990), 60.

[6] Foster and Smith, 7.

[7] Rev. Dr. Ken Orth, "Seasons of the Spirit: Prayer as Listening," https://fcc-winchester.com/latest-news/seasons-of-the-spirit-prayer-as-listening/ (accessed February 8, 2021).

presence, to lose ourselves in his redeeming purposes so we can find ourselves. Prayer is a sacred journey that guides us into becoming the people we were meant to become. As Jesus said, "A disciple is not above his teacher, but everyone who is fully trained will be like his teacher" (Luke 6:40). Jesus wants to fully train us so we can become like him. God the Son graciously became human, so that, by grace, we become human again. Our humanity was marred in the garden when the first humans sinned, and our humanity was restored in another garden, where Jesus walked out of an empty tomb. Becoming truly human is the grace-guided process of God uniting us to the life of the resurrected Messiah, by the Holy Spirit's power, as we trust Jesus as our Savior. And little by little, day by day, year by year, we grow in reflecting the character, ministry, and mission of Jesus. All of life becomes God's playground to express the love of Jesus through us. Our lives become a praise song giving God the glory due his name.

PRAYER IS A HOLY LONGING TO BE WITH GOD, TO EXPERIENCE HIS LOVE THAT SURPASSES UNDERSTANDING, TO BE EMBRACED BY HIS MERCIFUL PRESENCE, TO LOSE OURSELVES IN HIS REDEEMING PURPOSES SO WE CAN FIND OURSELVES.

Prayer ushers us into greater depths of intimacy with the Father, the Son, and the Spirit. Intimacy means "into me you see." Prayer opens our eyes so we can behold the God of glory in the face of Jesus, "For God who said, 'Let light shine out of darkness,' has shone in our hearts to give the light of the knowledge of God's glory in the face of Jesus Christ" (2 Cor. 4:6). God wants us to see him, to be with him, and for him to be with us. He is Immanuel, the God who is with us (Matt. 1:23). He will be our God, and we will be his people.

Lord, Teach Us to Pray

We are going to learn and inhabit a life of prayer. Jesus mastered the art of prayer because he is the Master. Now, he wants to enroll us in his school of prayer.

Don't worry about passing or failing his class. Jesus already scored 100 percent for us through his sinless life, sacrificial death on the cross, and resurrection. He is patient. He is kind. He is tender with us. And he knows that there is no final exam that we must study to get our score that we must achieve. The aim of prayer is sweet fellowship with our Father God, who is an endless well of beauty, glory, grace, and love. This school lasts for more than a semester; prayer is an eternal gift of intimacy with God.

When we wonder if God is really listening to us or if he really hears us, we can find confidence in learning from this prayer that God always answers. One day Jesus was praying, and his disciples asked him to teach them to pray. He said:

> "Therefore you should pray like this:
> 'Our Father in heaven
> your name be honored as holy.
> Your kingdom come.
> Your will be done on earth
> as it is in heaven.
> Give us today our daily bread.
> And forgive us our debts,

as we also have forgiven our debtors.
And do not bring us into temptation,
but deliver us from the evil one.'"
(Matt. 6:9–13)

In AD 250, Cyprian, a North African pastor, is credited with coming up with the phrase, "The Lord's Prayer."[8] Like a diamond, which has multifaceted beauty, depending on the angle you see it, the Lord's Prayer also teaches us a multifaceted kingdom-of-God reality.

First, the Lord's Prayer is a mini catechism that teaches you about the Person and work of Christ Jesus.[9] Each line of this ancient prayer details an aspect of Jesus' life.

Second, you will discover that the Lord's Prayer is not about getting stuff from God, but about becoming who you were created to be. Your purpose, your passion, and your participation in God's kingdom will be ignited.

Third, you will approach God's throne of grace and mercy with boldness and confidence because you will pray the prayer that Jesus told you his Papa would hear and answer. When you pray the Lord's Prayer, you are praying God's will for your life.

Fourth, you will learn that God answers the Lord's Prayer in unexpected ways and at unexpected times. Sometimes the prayers we have prayed in silence with tears streaming down our face take years to be fulfilled. When a farmer plants seeds, he does not expect

---

[8] R. J. Utley, *The First Christian Primer: Matthew*, vol. 9 (Marshall, TX: Bible Lessons International, 2000), 53.

[9] A catechism is a summary of Christian doctrine with questions and answers. It is used as a means of teaching the Christian faith.

them to grow overnight. He knows that harvest time is coming. This book that I am writing is a seed that was planted in 2000.

The book is written in five sections:

Section I: Discovering Who Our Father Is

"Our Father in heaven, your name be honored as holy" (Matt. 6:9). We will spend time mining the rich treasure chest of Scripture, exploring who our Father in heaven is. As we discover our Father's love, faithfulness, redemptive purpose, and glory, we will experience our trust in him increasing.

Section II: Discovering God's Kingdom and Your Priestly Role in It

"Your kingdom come. Your will be done on earth as it is in heaven" (v. 10). *The better we know and understand Abba's kingdom and our priestly role in it, the more purposeful and fulfilling our life of prayer will be.* As we walk through this section, we will discover what it means to:

- Participate in the kingdom
- Proclaim the kingdom
- Personify the kingdom
- Pursue the kingdom

Prayer is not making stuff up as we go along. Prayer is us reminding ourselves of what Abba has already accomplished in and through Jesus. The kingdom of God is what Jesus looks like in bodily form, and our priestly role in God's kingdom is to be formed into the image of Jesus. Prayer is rehearsing God's story and how we fit into it, for his glory.

PRAYER IS REHEARSING GOD'S STORY AND HOW WE FIT INTO IT, FOR HIS GLORY.

Section III: Depending on the Bread of Life

"Give us today our daily bread" (v. 11). As the Bread of Life, we will come to embrace Jesus as our provider. He is our breadwinner. He alone sustains us with the sustenance of his being. Jesus cares about the whole of our lives, not just souls. He graciously meets our every need we have at every level of our being.

Section IV: Diving into God's Forgiveness

"And forgive us our debts, as we also have forgiven our debtors" (v. 12). Section IV is going to be bloody. We are going to explore two of ancient Israel's holiest days, Passover and Yom Kippur. We learn that Jesus is the new Passover Lamb and our eternal Yom Kippur. Jesus frees us from the power of sin and death and forgives us so we can become forgivers. Unresolved forgiveness often dissolves our potential.

Section V: Developing a Wartime Mindset

"And do not bring us into temptation, but deliver us from the evil one" (v. 13). As this section unfolds, we will discover that Jesus holds us in his vast strength. No temptation is too great because we will learn how to put on Christ and resist temptation (Rom. 13:14). We will put on our battle armor because we are in a war. And in this war, God has given us special armor to wear so we can be effective in our already promised victory (Eph. 6:10–20).

God, do you hear me?

There is no one holy like the LORD.
There is no one besides you!
And there is no rock like our God.
(1 Sam. 2:2)

———————— Marinate on This ————————

Prayer

Heavenly Father,

Teach me to pray.

I long to learn.

I confess that most of the time I pray just to get things.

Rarely do I pray to get you.

Rarely do I pray simply to be with you.

Today, I choose to enroll in your school of prayer.

Teach me, O God, how to pray.

In Jesus' name, who is the Lord of Life,

And the One who gives me access to your ear,

Thank you for hearing me.

Amen.

Questions for Reflection

1. In what way do our lives look like the children building sandcastles on the beach?

2. What promise does Jesus make to those who build their lives on his teaching?

3. What is the goal of prayer? How is that different than what often motivates us to pray?

4. What are you most looking forward to about the rest of this book?

Things to Remember

1. We often find ourselves racked with anxiety, exhaustion, bitterness, and frustration because the sandcastles we have worked so hard to build are wiped away by the rising tides and cruel waves that crash on our lives.

2. As we have realized the world around us is in desperate need of redemption, our behavior reminds us that the interior part of our lives is also in need of redemption. What is in us is, by far, worse than what is outside of us.

3. Prayer is a sacred journey that guides us into becoming the people we were meant to become.

4. Like a diamond, which has multifaceted beauty, depending on the angle you see it, the Lord's Prayer also teaches us a multifaceted kingdom-of-God reality.

Discovering Who Our Father Is

"Our Father in heaven, your name be honored as holy."
MATTHEW 6:9

In this section, we will spend time mining the rich treasure chest of Scripture, exploring who our Father in heaven is. As we discover our Father's love, faithfulness, redemptive purpose, and glory, we will experience our trust in him increasing.

CHAPTER 2

Our Father Is Loving

Can you imagine a world drowning in fear, anxiety, and hopelessness?

Can you picture a place where sexual immorality, racism, and addiction run rampant?

Imagine waking up to a community ravaged by war, poverty, and systemic injustice?

I suspect you're saying, "Derwin, I'm living in twenty-first-century America. I *am* living in this world."

Our world and the first-century world of Jesus are not that much different in these ways. Ever since that fatal attraction in the garden of Eden, humanity has been fatally attracted to sin, resulting in death. "Therefore," wrote the apostle Paul, "just as sin entered the world through one man, and death through sin, in this way death spread to all people, because all sinned" (Rom. 5:12).

The World of Jesus

When Jesus was born more than 2,000 years ago, the Jewish people were anticipating the arrival of the Messiah, whom the sacred Scriptures prophesied would come. They believed that this Messiah would invade the Promised Land and rid it of the oppressive Romans. They wondered, "How could Israel be the great nation God promised, yet be occupied by Gentiles?" The Roman Empire had conquered Israel and ruled the Jewish people with a cruel fist of oppression. So, the Messiah would come and undo this oppression, ruling with an iron fist of his own.

As a little boy, Jesus would have been familiar with the sight of Jewish men hanging on crosses as he walked the Judean highways. The cross was not simply designed to kill. It was also a sign of intimidation and a political and theological symbol. It let the Jewish people know who was politically in charge—Caesar. It was also a sign that proclaimed that the Roman pantheon of gods was greater than Israel's God, Yahweh.

As a result of unmet expectations, and the regular reminders that their Messiah had still not come to redeem them, many of the Jews were angry and felt abandoned. They believed that God had not fulfilled his covenant with Abraham, thus failing to make them a great nation as promised (see Gen. 12:1–3; Heb. 11:8–10).

Learning to See the Invisible

Like the Jews of old, we, too, cry out, "God, where are you? Can you hear us? We, your people of promise in Messiah Jesus, need your divine deliverance." As we inhabit this mess, we must learn how to see the un-see-able: "But hope that is seen is not hope, because who hopes for what he sees? Now if we hope for what we do not see, we eagerly wait for it with patience" (Rom. 8:24–25). We must ask God to give us eyes that can see in the dark so we can perceive his invisible kingdom of light.

WE MUST ASK GOD TO GIVE US EYES THAT CAN SEE IN THE DARK SO WE CAN PERCEIVE HIS INVISIBLE KINGDOM OF LIGHT.

Learning to cultivate a life of prayer opens our eyes to see God's kingdom all around us. Dallas Willard, a wise, faithful believer of Jesus, wrote,

> We live in a Trinitarian universe, one where infinite energy of a personal nature is ultimate reality. When we pray, we enter the real world, the substance of the kingdom, and our bodies and souls begin to function for the first time as they were created.[1]

Learning to pray is of epic importance. Discovering how to pray is like finding out our lungs were made for oxygen. It is what God uses to give us night-time vision so we can see his kingdom in the midst of a dark world.

We were made for prayer—and prayer makes us.

The School of Prayer

One day Jesus was praying in a certain place. Stop for a moment and reread that sentence—Jesus prayed. Even now, Jesus is praying for us: "Christ Jesus is the one who died, but even more, has been raised; he also is at the right hand of God and intercedes for us" (Rom. 8:34).

---

[1] Dallas Willard, *The Divine Conspiracy* (San Francisco: HarperOne, 1997), 254.

Why would Jesus pray, you might ask? Many of us have wondered about this. After all, isn't Jesus God? So why would he need to pray?

Jesus prayed because he loved his Abba (Father) and his Abba loved him. *Abba* is the Aramaic term Jesus used to describe God the Father. Abba is a word that expresses great love and respect. Prayer is how Jesus sustained a life of intimacy with God the Father. For Jesus—and for us, as we will see—prayer isn't about getting God to give you stuff. Only with that misguided understanding of prayer will we wonder why Jesus prayed. But if prayer is about intimacy with God the Father, then it makes perfect sense why Jesus, the beloved Son, would pray.

After seeing Jesus pray, the disciples asked him, "Lord, teach us to pray" (Luke 11:1). So Jesus said to them,

> "Therefore, you should pray like this:
> 'Our Father in heaven,
> your name be honored as holy.
> Your kingdom come.
> Your will be done
> on earth as it is in heaven.
> Give us today our daily bread
> And forgive us our debts,
> as we also have forgiven our debtors.
> And do not bring us into temptation
> but deliver us from the evil one.'"
> (Matt. 6:9–13)

This is the prayer God hears. This is the prayer God answers. This is the prayer we were created to live.

Do you remember the first day of high school? I do. Several other freshmen and I walked about a mile to the bus stop with some upperclassmen. The upperclassmen knew what to expect. We did not. *Would I be able to find my locker? Would I be able to find my homeroom?* I'm so glad the upperclassmen told us what to expect and even helped us find out where to go that first day.

Learning to pray is a lot like our first day of high school. Jesus is the Master Teacher, and the disciples knew to ask him how to pray. But we also need upperclassmen in Jesus' school of prayer to help us. People who have walked in the way of Christ for longer than we have. My upperclassman is Vicki Gray. She is my wife, best friend, and ministry partner. Besides Jesus, my wife has taught me more about prayer than anyone. I have read about how the giants of the faith prayed, but I have seen Vicki pray day after day, month after month, year after year. I have had a front-row seat in her classroom.

I have watched her pray fighting cancer.

I have witnessed her pray as we co-planted Transformation Church.

I have seen her pray in the midst of crippling depression.

I have been awed by how she has taught the Transformation Church staff to pray. Our staff and church are a house of prayer, and God the Holy Spirit has used her as the architect. This I know—when I wake up in the morning and walk downstairs to get my morning coffee, I will find Vicki praying with Bible open and Mr. Boots, our lovable twenty-pound cat, by her side. Vicki is an overcomer because she has, in response to the deep love of Jesus, cultivated a life of prayer.

Prayer 101

In the Lord's Prayer, the very first thing Jesus does is call God "our Father." This is the introduction to his school of prayer.

Truthfully, I struggled with this because I did not have much of a relationship with my own father. As one of my teammates with the Indianapolis Colts was sharing Jesus with me in the mid-1990s, he kept saying, "Your Father in heaven loves you." I wondered, "How can God be a father in heaven who loves me when I am not sure my father, who lived a few blocks away, loves me?" When I discovered how loving my heavenly Father was, I was able to reconcile with and love my earthly father.

Love is an essential attribute of who God is. Just as God is eternal, he has eternally loved you. There has never been a moment that God has not loved you. He loved you before there were moments. His love for you stretches from eternity past to eternity present.

Even at your worst, God loved you: "But God proves his own love for us in that while we were still sinners, Christ died for us" (Rom. 5:8).

THERE HAS NEVER BEEN A MOMENT THAT GOD HAS NOT LOVED YOU.

We sing with King David, "My lips will glorify you because your faithful love is better than life" (Ps. 63:3). Our Abba wants us to know him. As we get familiar with him and his ways of grace, we will want to spend more time in prayer.

If we want to know what God is like, all we must do is look at Jesus. Jesus is the human face of God, "For God who said, 'Let light shine out of darkness,' has shone in our hearts to give the light of the knowledge of God's glory in the face of Jesus Christ" (2 Cor. 4:6). Jesus is "the radiance of God's glory and the exact expression of his nature, sustaining all things by his powerful word" (Heb. 1:3). As Jesus taught his disciples to pray, he started with "Our Father in heaven." Jesus shows us that God is loving by how he loved people and the stories he told.

What Is Our Father in Heaven Like?

Jesus told a story that painted a picture of what the Father is like. In the passage, known as the Story of the Prodigal Son, we see a love-sick father running to embrace his sinful, shame-filled son (Luke 15:11–32).

A Jewish father had two sons. The younger son asked his father for his share of the estate. In a shame and honor culture like the first-century Jewish world, his request was like spitting in his daddy's face. The younger son basically said, "Dad, you're worth more to me dead than alive."

However, the father gave the younger son his one-third of the estate, but his son sold his share. To add greater shame to his father, he then went to the land of the Gentiles and lived foolishly, squandering everything. He found himself penniless, so he takes a job at a pig farm. He was so hungry he wanted to eat the pig's food. Not only was his money gone, but so was his self-respect. This is what sin does—it dehumanizes us.

It is often in the brokenness that results from our own sinful choices, that we wake up to the whisper of our Abba saying, "Come home, precious child. I have never stopped loving you." The son remembered that his father's servants have enough food to eat. It was then that he came to his senses and prepared to go home.

While the son was a long way off, his daddy saw him, and his heart overflowed with compassion. The father took off on a full sprint to his son. When he reached him, he threw himself on his son, hugging and kissing him. The father ran to his son because, according to Jewish custom, if a son disgraced his father, village elders would stop the son before he reached home. They would then smash a pot at the son's feet, symbolizing his banishment from that community.[2] The father hurried so he could outrun the village elders to his baby boy. The father sprinted with love in his heart. The village elders ran with condemnation in their hands. When the father hugged and kissed his son, he was saying, "If you smash the pot of banishment on him, you must smash it on me too."

Now it was the father who was making himself undignified— not because of his lavish sin, like his son, but because of his lavish love.

Our Abba sent Jesus running to the cross.

The pot of sin, shame, guilt, and condemnation was smashed on Jesus, instead of on us.

When we were utterly helpless, Christ came at just the right time and died for us sinners (Rom. 5:6).

After the father embraced his son, he immediately told his servants to get the best robe, a ring, sandals, and a fattened calf. "It is time to celebrate my son coming back home. My son was dead, but now he is alive. He was lost, but now he is found."

---

[2] Scot McKnight, *The Jesus Creed* (Brewster, MA: Paraclete Press, 2004), 29–30.

The robe covered the son's filth. Abba covers our filth by clothing us in the robe of Christ's righteousness (Gal. 3:26–27).

The ring restored the son's authority as an heir. Abba restores us as coheirs with Jesus.

The shoes meant the son was no longer a slave. Abba gives us the gospel of peace on our feet, so we are no longer slaves to sin and death. We are Abba's kids.

We were dead. But in Abba's mercy and great love, he made us alive in Christ.

We were lost. But by Abba's grace, he found us and welcomed us home.

When the father requested a fattened lamb, he is throwing a party, celebrating the return of his son. God sings and dances over us. Jesus is the lamb that was given so our Abba could welcome us home.

JESUS IS THE LAMB THAT WAS GIVEN SO OUR ABBA COULD WELCOME US HOME.

The Older Brother

However, the story doesn't end there. The father had an older son who stayed home and refused to celebrate his little brother's return. As the celebration was going on, the father spoke to his older son outside of the party. The older brother compared himself to his younger brother and reminded his dad all that he had done for him, how hard he had worked, and all the ways his little brother had disgraced the family (Luke 15:29–30).

If the older brother understood grace, he would have understood that he could only do what he did for his father because the father gave him the ability and access to do it. If the older brother understood grace, he would have been amazed and in awe of how gracious his father was to his brother. If the older brother understood grace, he would have been celebrating his brother's return from the dead. If the older brother understood grace, he would have known that he did not have to work for what his father had already given him.

How sad it is that the older brother stayed home but did not know that the house was his. Even though he stayed, he was dead, lost, and just as far away from home as his little brother. Both sons were lost. One was lost in self-loathing and sin. The other was lost in pride and sin. Both missed the love of their father. However, one woke up to his father's love and came back home.

Come home. And do not leave Abba's house.

—————————— **Marinate on This** ——————————

Prayer

Abba,

I have been created by your love to experience your love.

Often, I feel unlovable, but you say I am loved
with a divine love that is limitless.

Lord Jesus,

When the winds of doubt turn my face

Remind me of your grace.

Remind me that the cross is your forever "I love you."

Holy Spirit,

Help me to remember that I am one of Abba's kids.

Help me to draw life from Abba's unceasing love in Christ Jesus.

May the love I live in be the love I give to others.

Amen.

Questions to Reflect On

1. Do you ever feel like the first-century Jews in Jesus' day—
   wondering where God is and why he's not doing something
   about all the chaos and brokenness in the world?

2. How does prayer help us see the light of God's kingdom in a dark world?

3. Who are the upperclassmen in prayer you can look to for help and mentorship?

4. What did you learn from the story of the father and his two sons? How does this story highlight God's love for his wayward children?

Things to Remember

1. We must ask God to give us eyes that can see in the dark so we can perceive his invisible kingdom of light.

2. In the Lord's Prayer, the very first thing Jesus does is call God "Our Father." This is the introduction to his school of prayer.

3. If we want to know what God is like, all we must do is look at Jesus. Jesus is the human face of God.

4. Jesus is the lamb that was given so our Abba could welcome us home.

CHAPTER 3

Our Father Is Sovereign

 The more we know our Father in heaven, the more we will want to pray. As we learn about his character, we'll grow more fond of him, and desire to spend more time with him. The good news for us is, God has chosen to reveal himself to us in his Word. We know exactly where to go to learn more about him. So, let's embark on an exploration of what theologians call God's attributes.

Even though we are born in different places, at different times, and under different circumstances, there is a common thread that binds us together. We all have a story.

Perhaps, like me, your parents did not plan for you to be born. But God always *had* a plan for you (Acts 17:26). Before your dad met your mom and could not resist her smile, God loved you. Before your DNA gave its exquisite genetic instructions to form your tiny hands, your beating heart, and your perfect eyes, God knew you (Ps. 139:14). You may have been an accident to your parents. But you are no accident. You were created *by* divine purpose *for* a divine purpose.

YOU WERE CREATED BY DIVINE PURPOSE FOR A DIVINE PURPOSE.

Our Father in heaven is sovereign. This means God is working through the actions of humans to accomplish his purposes, to eventually redeem, restore, and heal all of creation and those who trust in his eternal Son, King Jesus. God will "bring everything together in Christ, both things in heaven and things on earth in him" (Eph. 1:10). Ultimately, God's sovereignty is expressed in the redeeming work of Jesus and his blood.

> For God was pleased to have all his fullness dwell in him, and through him to reconcile everything to himself, whether things on earth or things in heaven, by making peace through his blood, shed on the cross. (Col. 1:19–20)

The One who hears our prayers is the sovereign One.

When we pray "Our Father," we are praying to our sovereign Creator, the One who has eternally loved us with unmatched tenderness; the One who holds us with unparalleled strength. Our Father in heaven crafted us with infinite care and precision. Before we ever looked in the mirror and recognized our face, *El-Roi*, the God who sees (Gen. 16:13), eternally saw us. When you feel forgotten and unseen, our Father sees you. You are known. There is nothing random about you or your life.

> Before a word is on my tongue, you know all about it, LORD. You have encircled me; you have placed your hand on me. This wondrous knowledge is beyond me. It is lofty; I am unable to reach it. (Ps. 139:4–6)

God knows the end from the beginning (Isa. 46:10). Jesus is "the Alpha and the Omega, the first and the last, the beginning and the end" (Rev. 22:13); "He is before all things, and by him, all things hold together" (Col. 1:17). God the Holy Spirit "knows the thoughts of God" because he is God (1 Cor. 2:11). When we pray, "Our Father," in Jesus' name, through the Spirit's power, we are praying to our eternal creator, who is all-seeing, all-knowing, all-powerful, and all-loving. He is worthy of our allegiance.

> You made all the delicate, inner parts of my body and knit me together in my mother's womb. . . . You saw me before I was born. Every day of my life was recorded in your book. Every moment was laid out before a single day had passed. (Ps. 139:13, 16 NLT)

If God Knows, Why Pray?

If God knows everything, why should we pray? If he is sovereign, what's the point?

This question assumes that prayer is like making wishes to a genie in a bottle—but we do not pray like that. That approach is the problem with the American Gospel where Jesus has become a consumer good instead of a good God whom we serve for his glory. Jesus did not go to the cross and rise from the dead to serve us like a butler. He rose from the dead "so that he would be the firstborn among many brothers and sisters" who embody the kingdom of God on earth as it is in heaven (Rom. 8:29). Jesus restores our divine birthright as "a chosen race, a royal priesthood, a holy nation, a people for his possession, so that [we] may proclaim the praises of the one who called [us] out of darkness into his marvelous light" (1 Pet. 2:9).

JESUS DID NOT GO TO THE CROSS AND RISE FROM THE DEAD TO SERVE US LIKE A BUTLER.

We pray because we love him and want to know him more.

We pray because we want to experience his beautiful life-giving presence.

We pray because we want to inhabit the world as God's people on God's mission for God's glory.

Abba is un-surprise-able, but he will surprise us when he invites us into his kingdom. Like the loving parent he is, God patiently teaches us through the Holy Spirit *how to live* in a new and better story of grace as citizens and royal priests in his kingdom. We needed a better story, so God, out of an endless ocean of love, gave us Jesus' story. God rescued "us from the domain of darkness and transferred us into the kingdom of the Son he loves" (Col. 1:13).

Jesus' life, Jesus' story, and Jesus' achievements are forever ours, by grace through faith (Col. 3:3–4).

We have been transferred into Jesus' kingdom. We have a new zip code. We are relocated in the Messiah Jesus. This is our new story. As we learn the Lord's Prayer, we are learning Jesus' story and how we fit in it. As we learn the Lord's Prayer, we are discovering our destiny.

We Needed a Better Story

Life in a fallen world brings us mountaintop seasons of happiness and long valleys of great sadness. These moments are like train tracks running side-by-side in our souls. Happiness, sadness, flourishing, failure, sin—all comingled together like our bones, ligaments, and blood.

No one is *story-free. And no one is free from their stories.*

Our stories keep us locked inside our homes like a child being punished. All we can do is press our little faces against the window and wish we could go outside and play with our friends. We can see freedom, but we cannot experience it.

Why? Because we were born locked in the domain of darkness (Rom. 5:12). We inherited the sin-sickness from the first Adam's DNA. We need to be reborn and inherit the life-giving DNA of the last Adam, Jesus Christ (1 Cor. 15:45; John 3:5). We need a better story that flings open the door so we can run out and play. By his death and resurrection Jesus tore the hinges off the door so we could go outside with the rest of Abba's kids in the fresh air of his kingdom.

The first Adam gave us a story of death. The last Adam gave us a story of life (1 Cor. 15:22). Our first womb was a spiritual tomb. But Jesus' tomb became a life-giving womb.

> But God is so rich in mercy, and he loved us so much, that even though we were dead because of our sins, he gave us life when he raised Christ from the dead. (It is only by God's grace that you have been saved!) For he raised us from the dead along with Christ and seated us with him in the heavenly realms because we are united with Christ Jesus. (Eph. 2:4–6 NLT)

Jesus lives in you. He has re-written your story with his story of resurrection life. You are a partaker in the life of King Jesus.

> Now if Christ is in you, the body is dead because of sin, but the Spirit gives life because of righteousness. And if the Spirit of him who raised Jesus from the dead lives in you, then he who raised Christ from the dead will also bring your mortal bodies to life through his Spirit who lives in you. (Rom. 8:10–11)

Sadly, so many of Abba's kids embrace Jesus' forgiveness while neglecting his life within them. Telling a dead person that they are forgiven does not help the dead person. They cannot hear or feel the power of forgiveness. But if the dead person can be made alive, then the words "You are forgiven" become a healing balm. When Jesus wipes away our sins, he imparts his life to us. Abba's kids are alive with the life of heaven on earth (John 1:12). When we pray "Our Father," we are praying to the One who re-creates us into a forgiven, alive-with-the-life-of-Christ family. We are born a second time. A miracle takes place. We have a new and better story.

God's Sovereign Handwriting in My Life

I grew up on the west side of San Antonio, Texas. My sixteen-year-old mom fought to bring me into the world. My seventeen-year-old dad dropped out of high school so he could work and provide for his new family. Both my mom and dad had various struggles.

After elementary school, I primarily lived with my grandparents on my mom's side. My grandfather, William E. Gilliam, aka Willie, was the hardest working man I have ever known. He had a little convenience store in the hood called *Willie's Quick Mart*. He worked every day. Without saying much, he taught me a lot. He taught me that a man works to provide for his family. There are mouths to feed and bills to be paid.

My grandmother, Ossie B. Gilliam, our "Gran Dune-Buggy" as I affectionately called her, had a special relationship with me. She was an incredible woman. We spoke nearly every day. When my grandmother died in 2005, her body was riddled with cancer. The beautiful, tall, strong woman was ravaged by this heinous disease. Watching someone die that you love kills a part of you. I spent time with her in Texas for two weeks as she was dying and praying to see Jesus face-to-face.

After two weeks, I needed to get back home to my wife and kids in Charlotte. By this time, she was in and out of consciousness. Early in the morning, the last time I would see her alive on this side of eternity, I had packed my bags and was slowly walking to the door. I looked back at her for what I knew would be the last time, and she raised up and, in crystal clear words, said, "Dewey, I am so proud of the husband and father you have become. I love you." Then she laid back down. My grandmother blessed me one last time.

I Have Scars Too

All of my life was not blessings, however. I have scars just like you. Some of my scars you can see. Other scars go beyond my skin and are branded in my soul. Scars tell a story, too.

I have witnessed the horrors of domestic violence.

I was molested as a little boy.

I was sexually immoral.

I lied to survive.

Like you, I was born into sin and sinned because I was born.

No one escapes scars in a world that has been fundamentally scarred by the dark power called sin. We all give and receive them. Despite my accomplishments of being the first college graduate in my family and having a successful professional football career, my story of rags-to-riches and my self-help motivational mantras could not heal my scars. My soul was constantly longing for what no one and no thing could provide.

My wife could not love me enough to heal me. No amount of money was ever enough to heal me. Winning the 1994 *RCA Man of the Year* for the Indianapolis Colts as a result of my community service and having October 14, 1996, declared *Derwin Gray Day* in the city of Indianapolis for community service were not enough to remove the guilt and shame I felt.

I needed a new story.

On August 2, 1997, I met Jesus in a small dorm room in Indiana at Anderson University. This moment is when I realized Jesus had scars, too. Jesus showed me his scars—his nail-pierced hands, the hole in his side, and the deep gashes on his head from the crown of thorns.

His scars told me that he loved me. They became my story of redemption. All my pain, shame, and guilt were placed in his flesh so I could taste and see that Abba is good.

ALL MY PAIN, SHAME, AND GUILT WERE PLACED IN JESUS' FLESH SO I COULD TASTE AND SEE THAT ABBA IS GOOD.

It was my fifth training camp with the Indianapolis Colts. As I walked to my dorm room after lunch, even though I had just eaten a meal, I was still hungry. The hunger pains of my soul could not be satisfied with physical food.

I was hungry for the Bread of Life.

I was thirsty for Living Water.

I needed Jesus.

I needed a story that was not written by me and my performance.

I needed a new and better story written by Jesus and his performance.

When I got back to my dorm room, I picked up the phone and called Vicki. I told her, "I want to be more committed to you. And I want to be committed to Jesus." As I said those words, I literally felt Abba's love pour over me like I was standing under a waterfall. For several nights after giving my allegiance to Jesus, I just cried and cried as I went to bed, thinking, *How could someone love me like this?* I am crying as I recall this moment. Paul's words ring true in my heart:

> He predestined us to be adopted as sons through Jesus Christ for himself, according to the good pleasure of his will, to the praise of his glorious grace that he lavished on us in the Beloved One. In him we have redemption through his blood, the forgiveness of our trespasses, according to the riches of his grace that he richly poured out on us with all wisdom and understanding. (Eph. 1:5–8)

There it is. All who trust in Jesus receive a new story of glorious grace.

Our Abba is giddy about adopting us into his family through his Beloved Son. He adopts us so we can become a living praise song, bearing witness to his glorious grace, which was lavished on us in his beloved Son, Jesus.

We all have a story, but in Abba's Beloved Son, your story and my story become Jesus' story. The blood of the Beloved Son breaks the story of sin and death with a new one of forgiveness and life. This is God who hears us. The God who answers us. The God who cherishes us. He is our sovereign Father.

Even the Bad Becomes Good

Because of the redemption we have in Christ, our scars now bear witness to God's sovereign love. In God's sovereign compassion, our scars become testimonies. What we thought was meant to break us, Abba uses to make us.

> You planned evil against me; God planned it for good to bring about the present result—the survival of many people. (Gen. 50:20)

It is an astonishingly beautiful thing that God is working in and using all things—not some things but *all* things—to form the image of the Messiah in his children:

> We know that all things work together for the good of those who love God, who are called according to his purpose. For those he foreknew he also predestined to be conformed to the image of his Son, so that he would be the firstborn among many brothers and sisters. (Rom. 8:28–29)

You may have a hard time believing that. *Really, Derwin? All things? You don't know about the bad stuff that's happened to me. Surely there's some stuff that is outside of God's control.*

But believe it or not, even the worst atrocity in human history—the murder of Jesus—became the means of redeeming humanity and all of creation. Let the sovereign presence and power of Abba comfort you:

> "Fellow Israelites, listen to these words: This Jesus of Nazareth was a man attested to you by God with miracles, wonders, and signs that God did among you through him, just as you yourselves know. Though he was delivered up according to God's determined plan and foreknowledge, you used lawless people to nail him to a cross and kill him. God raised him up, ending the pains of death, because it was not possible for him to be held by death." (Acts 2:22–24)

If God can bring the greatest good in the history of creation out of the greatest evil in the history of creation, surely he can work together everything in our lives for our good!

When we pray "Our Father," we are praying to our loving, sovereign Abba, who invites us into Jesus' story of redemption. We, as Abba's Spirit-empowered kids, become his sovereign means by which he heals and restores people and all of creation, from the tiniest atom to the greatest ocean. All things will be made new.

> For we know that all creation has been groaning as in the pains of childbirth right up to the present time. And we believers also groan, even

though we have the Holy Spirit within us as a foretaste of future glory, for we long for our bodies to be released from sin and suffering. We, too, wait with eager hope for the day when God will give us our full rights as his adopted children, including the new bodies he has promised us. (Rom. 8:22–23 NLT)

When we pray "Our Father," we are communing with our loving, sovereign creator, who holds us near his heart. Our Father's sovereign love means he is acting in wondrous and mysterious ways in history "to bring everything together in Christ, both things in heaven and things on earth in him" (Eph. 1:10).

Our Abba is great and unmatched in his glory, and he loves to hear his beloved children call his name.

——————— Marinate on This ———————

Prayer

Pray for family and friends using the framework of this prayer:

Abba,

in our world filled with chaos and uncertainty

I can be certain that, in Christ, you hold all things together.

You know the end from the beginning.

You are the first and you are the last.

Your presence is with me.

Your wisdom goes before me.

Your strength holds me.

The life of Christ is my source of life.

I can trust you.

In your sovereign love, you take the bad
and use it to make us good.

Even creation itself will be made new in your sovereign hands.

Even when we cannot understand and ambiguity clouds our vision,

we know, Abba, by the Spirit's power, you
bring all things together in Christ.

I trust you.

In Jesus' name, amen.

God, do you hear me?

Questions to Reflect On

1. Why is it important for us to study the attributes of God if we want our prayer life to improve?

2. What does it mean that God is sovereign?

3. Why is God's sovereignty good news for your life and mine?

4. How does the promise that God works all things—the good and the bad—together for the good of his children bring you comfort? Where in your life right now do you need to believe that promise?

Things to Remember

1. Our Father in heaven is sovereign. This means God is working through the actions of humans to accomplish his purposes, to eventually redeem, restore, and heal all of creation and those who trust in his eternal Son, King Jesus.

2. When we pray "Our Father," we are praying to the One who re-creates us into a forgiven, alive-with-the-life-of-Christ family.

3. In God's sovereign compassion, our scars become testimonies. What we thought was meant to break us, Abba uses to make us.

4. The worst atrocity in human history—the murder of Jesus—became the means of redeeming humanity and all of creation.

CHAPTER 4

Our Father Is Holy

I am a fanboy of Vicki Gray. I love my wife. Her strength inspires me. Her courage makes me brave, and her allegiance to Jesus moves my heart to become a better man. She parents our children with wisdom and grace. She leads at Transformation Church, which we cofounded in 2010, with a sense of urgency that is beautifully directed by the Holy Spirit. She's pretty much what Wonder Woman would be like in real life.

My admiration for her has grown as I have watched her *live out* her faith as she battled thyroid cancer, two hard pregnancies with hyperemesis gravidarum—which is nine months of vomiting—a heartbreaking miscarriage, and depression. I am further inspired by the way she has loved me, our kids, and those she disciples through it all.

I met Vicki on February 15, 1990, when we were student-athletes at Brigham Young University (BYU). In the beautiful mystery of God's sovereignty, I found myself walking into the weight room where the athletes trained. It was odd that no other athletes were there lifting weights, except this beautiful, muscular girl with a long ponytail. Vicki was doing a lift called triceps extensions. Her triceps were ripped, and I thought to myself, *Dang! I hope she asks me for a spot*. As that thought made itself comfortable in mind, she said, "Can you give me a spot?" I was trying to be cool, but on the inside, my heart was beating out of my chest. After she completed her lift, she thanked me, and was on to the next exercise.

A few weeks went by before I saw her playing basketball. She was throwing elbows in dudes' ribs and knocking down three-point shots like Steph Curry. After her display of athleticism, I had to meet this warrior girl. In an act of courage like the world has never seen, I enlisted my football teammate Rick Wilson to ask her if I could talk with her after the game. The next thing I knew, we were in the bleachers having a conversation. She told me that she was on the BYU track team, and she threw the javelin. I was equally terrified and attracted to this Amazon warrior. Vicki told me she had a boyfriend, so I backed off. But then, a few weeks later, I saw the girl with the long ponytail and ripped triceps walking down the hall near the BYU weight room. "You still have a boyfriend?" I asked. She said "no," and thirty years later, we're still together.

Vicki is the love of my life, my best friend, and my ministry partner. But before I met her, she had already lived part of her story, which Jesus would re-write one day.

Small Town Girl with Big City Dreams

Vicki is from a small town called Darby, Montana. What it lacks in size, it makes up for in beauty. Nestled in the Bitterroot Valley of Western Montana, the surrounding mountains, such as Trapper's Peak, are breathtaking.

Vicki excelled academically and athletically in school. Her lowest GPA ever was 3.89, which happened to coincide with her meeting and dating me. She was valedictorian in high school and at BYU. She was driven. Everything she did, she had to be the best, and she was the best. She is so athletically gifted that one day in her freshman year at Darby High School, one of her coaches asked her to throw the javelin. She told him, "I'm not interested." He then challenged her to throw it, so she picked up the javelin and sailed it through the air. A few weeks later, she was the state champion in the sport.

Her first love, however, was basketball. She was an all-state player, and at one time, she had the state record for three-point shots made in a game with six. The small-town girl was doing *big* things. She wanted to attend a big university and leave her mark on the world. She decided to accept an academic and athletic scholarship to BYU.

External success is like putting on makeup. Makeup hides our facial flaws and raccoon eyes, but eventually, you have to wash it off and see your real face. Like me, like you, Vicki's makeup was her external performance. But her real face was one of a precious but broken girl who needed Abba's love, healing, and affirmation.

Vicki started drinking in middle school. Drinking is a way of life in Montana. There are more bars than churches in Darby. By the time she got to college, her drinking and partying days were behind her, but the toxic decisions that one makes while drinking were still with her. The scars of her past brought pain into her present reality.

Academic and athletic success could not heal her pain.

Being beautiful could not heal her pain.

Boyfriends could not heal her pain.

Being in peak physical condition could not heal her pain.

Underneath her high-level achieving, Vicki was a tender girl who was in the grips of an eating disorder, episodes of depression, and feelings of unworthiness.

Vicki and I were models of external success, but inside we were a mess.

We fell in love fast and were inseparable. To the shock of our parents, we got married in college on May 23, 1992. I rented a cheap tux, and Vicki borrowed a wedding dress. The assistant athletic director at BYU, Mike King, officiated our wedding. Our honeymoon was one night at the Marriott Hotel in downtown Provo. The next morning, I went to train with the BYU football team, and Vicki went to work.

We clicked so well together because we were both driven, ambitious, and hard-working. Like most people, we were born believing these traits could fix us. Drivenness is great if it is fueled by the Holy Spirit's power. Our drivenness was not.

WE WERE BOTH DRIVEN, AMBITIOUS, AND HARD-WORKING. LIKE MOST PEOPLE, WE WERE BORN BELIEVING THESE TRAITS COULD FIX US.

Ambition is good if it is for the glory of Abba. Our ambition was not.

Work ethic is epic if it flows out of the redemptive work of Jesus. Our work ethic did not.

It is impossible to live a supernatural life when your life is devoid of the supernatural God.

> And you were dead in your trespasses and sins
> in which you previously walked according to the
> ways of this world, according to the ruler of the

power of the air, the spirit now working in the
disobedient. (Eph. 2:1–2)

Abba Loves Messes

When we pray "Our Father in heaven," we are praying to a
Father that loves to step into our mess and clean us up. He hears us.

Vicki and I both had tremendous college experiences. People
loved us there. We were like Mr. and Mrs. BYU in 1992. But then
we moved to Indiana, where I was to play for the Indianapolis Colts,
and Vicki was to be an NFL player's wife. Our dreams quickly
turned into a nightmare.

A few of my black teammates were racist toward my white wife
and me.

Vicki became "Derwin's wife." She was used to being known
as Vicki.

I did not know how to love her. And she did not know how to
respect me.

Both of us were a hot mess. But then God jumped in the middle
of our mess.

In 1994, Vicki worked at Blackburn Health Clinic in urban
Indianapolis. She was a registered dietician, and, of course, she was
named the Young Dietician of the Year in the State of Indiana.

In his sovereign love, God had a missionary at Blackburn Health
Clinic named Karen. Vicki would frequently come home from work
and tell me about her and her kindness. As God the Holy Spirit was
working in Vicki's heart, she was prompted to ask Karen, "Do you
believe demons are real?" Karen said, "Yes." Some time went by, and
over coffee amid a busy health clinic, Karen asked Vicki if she was
a Christian. Vicki said, "Yes. I believe in God." Karen lovingly and

patiently said, "Being a Christian is more than believing in God. Being a Christian means that you have trusted Jesus to forgive your sins and that you believe he rose from the dead on the third day. It means you follow him." Vicki had a deer-in-the-headlights look on her face. But the gospel was tenderizing her heart.

On a cold, wintry Sunday morning, at a beautiful, gothic-looking Presbyterian church, Jesus called Vicki's name. She does not remember the sermon, but she does remember the choir singing the words, "And he died for me." Those words broke through and reached her heart. She grabbed our baby girl, Presley, and ran out of the church crying. As she drove home, all she could hear were the words, "And he died for me." This moment is when the God of life breathed *his* life into her. She was born-again. Vicki met the Lord of Life.

> In him was life, and that life was the light of men. That light shines in the darkness, and yet the darkness did not overcome it. (John 1:4–5)

> The one who has the Son has life. The one who does not have the Son of God does not have life. (1 John 5:12)

The love of Abba in Christ, by his Spirit, came to dwell in her. She became a new creation. Vicki loves butterflies because they represent transformation. In Christ, Vicki sees herself as Abba's beautiful butterfly, and so do I.

> This means that anyone who belongs to Christ has become a new person. The old life is gone; a new life has begun! (2 Cor. 5:17 NLT)

Our Father is the God of new creation. This is who we are praying to.

Face-to-Face with Holiness

The idea that Jesus would exchange his life for her life, given the guilt and shame she carried, captured her heart. Because she had been forgiven much, she loved Jesus much, and wanted to make much of him.

> "Therefore I tell you, her many sins have been forgiven; that's why she loved much. But the one who is forgiven little loves little." (Luke 7:47)

Vicki developed an insatiable appetite to know Jesus more. The more she knew him, the more she was becoming like him and wanting others to know him. Abba, through the Holy Spirit's power, took her same drive, ambition, and work ethic and now empowered it for Jesus' glory.

Early in Vicki's journey with Jesus, God's holiness made her even more appreciative of God's grace. This gratitude is called worship. Worship is simply a life lived in appreciation of God's mercy. A prayerful life is a worshipful life.

WORSHIP IS SIMPLY A LIFE LIVED IN APPRECIATION OF GOD'S MERCY. A PRAYERFUL LIFE IS A WORSHIPFUL LIFE.

Therefore, brothers and sisters, in view of the mercies of God, I urge you to present your bodies as

a living sacrifice, holy and pleasing to God; this is
your true worship. (Rom. 12:1)

God's holiness is the infinite, unrivaled love that the Father, the
Son, and the Holy Spirit have eternally shared and enjoyed. God's
holiness is his perfection, beauty, and purity. He is uncontaminated
by anything unclean, impure, or unjust. And he is perfectly unique,
different, and other than all he has created.

For the High and Exalted One, who lives forever,
whose name is holy, says this: "I live in a high and
holy place, and with the oppressed and lowly of
spirit, to revive the spirit of the lowly and revive
the heart of the oppressed." (Isa. 57:15)

In view of Abba's holiness, Vicki was humbled without being
humiliated and exalted without being elevated.

Because of Jesus' holiness, Vicki became infatuated with prayer.
As she experienced God's holy presence in prayer, she surrendered to
his guidance (Prov. 3:5–6). Vicki was becoming who she was meant
to be. She was becoming a Jesus Christ look-alike. Theologians call
this sanctification. I call it beautiful.

But as the one who called you is holy, you also are
to be holy in all your conduct; for it is written, Be
holy, because I am holy. (1 Pet. 1:15–16)

God invites us to share in his holiness. Otherwise, our impu-
rity, uncleanliness, and sin would keep us out of his loving presence
and holy family. When we are born again, we are eternally forgiven,
eternally alive with Christ, and clothed with his holiness. God

imparts his holiness to us as a gift, and we are empowered to a life holy or devoted to him and his kingdom.

God invites us to share in his holiness.

> God has united you with Christ Jesus. For our benefit God made him to be wisdom itself. Christ made us right with God; he made us pure and holy, and he freed us from sin. Therefore, as the Scriptures say, "If you want to boast, boast only about the LORD." (1 Cor. 1:30–31 NLT)

> For by that one offering he forever made perfect those who are being made holy. And the Holy Spirit also testifies that this is so. For he says, "This is the new covenant I will make with my people on that day, says the LORD: I will put my laws in their hearts, and I will write them on their minds." Then he says, "I will never again remember their sins and lawless deeds." (Heb. 10:14–17 NLT)

It is life-changing when we discover that the holiness that God requires of us is the gift he gives to us.

All It Takes Is One Glimpse

Vicki caught a glimpse of God's holiness. All it took was one look at his holy beauty, and her life was changed.

Several thousand years ago, there was a Jewish prophet named Isaiah, who also caught a glimpse of God's holy beauty (Isa. 6:1–2; John 12:41). He saw a vision of God's heavenly throne. It was a powerful, awesome, majestic scene that left Isaiah humbled and undone. The hem of God's robe filled the temple. The majestic seraphim, a class of powerful angels, were standing above him, calling out to each other, "Holy, holy, holy is the LORD of Armies; his glory fills the whole earth" (Isa. 6:3). The threefold repetition of "holy" signifies that God is infinitely holy, perfectly holy, as holy as possible.

Isaiah's vision corresponded with the Holy of Holies in the Jewish temple. The temple is where heaven and earth meet, where God's holy beauty meets God's people, atones for their sins, and sends them into the world to bear witness to his glory as missionaries.

Marinate with me for a moment: God, in his perfection, is so beautiful, so awesome, so great, all the mighty seraphim could do was shout to each other, "Holy, Holy, Holy, is the Yahweh! His glory fills the earth."

All it takes is one glimpse of God's holy beauty and we are changed. Isaiah saw the Lord in all his splendor and holiness. This was a holy and terrifying moment because Isaiah saw his sin and the sin of the people of Israel. In light of God's perfection, Isaiah knew without a doubt how imperfect he was. But God did not punish Isaiah; rather, the holy love of God in his pure, radiant, glory led Isaiah to repentance:

> Woe is me for I am ruined because I am a man of
> unclean lips and live among a people of unclean
> lips, and because my eyes have seen the King, the
> LORD of Armies. (Isa. 6:5)

Grace is not appreciated when the holiness of God is not valued. Isaiah says he is "ruined." He is unraveling at being in God's holy presence. He had seen the King, and the King's holiness brought him to his knees. This is a good thing because being on our knees is a sign of reverence. It is a living symbol of acknowledging God's infinite worth. It is only when we fall to our knees that he can pick us up.

Isaiah confesses his *personal* sin *and* the *corporate* sins of Israel. For us twenty-first-century American Christians, confessing sins that are not our own is a strange thing. It flies in the face of our rugged, Western individualism. But here, we see an example of Isaiah confessing the sins of God's people. It is a holy lamenting, a sign of solidarity with other believers, and a commitment to pray for and encourage brothers and sisters to not fall prey to the dark powers.

> Watch out, brothers and sisters, so that there won't be in any of you an evil, unbelieving heart that turns away from the living God. But encourage each other daily, while it is still called today, so that none of you is hardened by sin's deception. (Heb. 3:12–13)

Atonement for Sin

As Isaiah is melting under the holiness of God, he experiences our Father's grace as his sins are atoned for. This is what God in Christ Jesus did for us—atonement. To atone for sins means that by the blood of the unblemished lamb, the people's sin is forgiven and forgotten. Sins are wiped away. In Christ our sins are forgotten (Heb. 10:17). Atonement reconciles and restores our relationship with God. Abba, who is slow to anger, filled with mercy unending, overflowing in compassion, and loving to his children, sent his Son to atone for our sins.

**ATONEMENT RECONCILES AND
RESTORES OUR RELATIONSHIP
WITH GOD. ABBA, WHO IS SLOW
TO ANGER, FILLED WITH MERCY
UNENDING, OVERFLOWING IN
COMPASSION, AND LOVING TO
HIS CHILDREN, SENT HIS SON
TO ATONE FOR OUR SINS.**

Then one of the seraphim flew to me, and in his
hand was a glowing coal that he had taken from
the altar with tongs. He touched my mouth with
it and said: "Now that this has touched your lips,
your iniquity is removed and your sin is atoned
for." (Isa. 6:6–7)

After God atones for Isaiah's sin, God invites Isaiah into his
mission. Atonement is never just simply for us. Atonement forms us
into a missionary people. It is as if the river of God's love begins to
flow through us to water our parched souls. God wants to flood the
earth with his love for us to become overflowing rivers of his grace.
We see this in the next thing Isaiah said:

Then I heard the voice of the Lord asking: "Who
will I send? Who will go for us?" I said: "Here I
am. Send me." (Isa. 6:8)

The heavenly scene that Isaiah encounters grips my heart. In
response to God's atonement, Isaiah joins God's mission. There is
nothing like a heart that has encountered the holy beauty of God
and has become regenerated, remade, redirected, and repurposed for
God's mission to rescue people "from the domain of darkness and

[transfer them] into the kingdom of the Son he loves. In him we have redemption, the forgiveness of sins" (Col. 1:13–14).

Like the prophet Isaiah, Vicki caught a glimpse of God's holy glory, and it changed her life. The holy beauty of God can change your life, too. When we pray "Our Father in heaven," we are praying to One who is beautifully holy.

─────────── Marinate on This ───────────

Prayer

Abba,

You are high and exalted.

Holy is your name.

Your life spans from eternity past to eternity future.

All Glory and Power belong to you.

Your holiness is infinite.

You are perfect, beautiful, and pure.

Thank you,

That in Christ Jesus

Your holiness humbles me without humiliating me

And exalts me without elevating me.

The holiness you require is the holiness you give me as a gift.

May I go into the world with my eyes constantly gazing

upon your holy beauty, holy love,

as a Holy Spirit-filled missionary.

In Jesus' name, amen.

Questions to Reflect On

1. How has God stepped into your mess?

2. What does it mean that God is holy?

3. How should we respond to God's holiness?

4. Does the holiness of God make you eager to pray to him?

Things to Remember

1. When we pray "Our Father in heaven," we are praying to a Father who loves to step into our mess and clean us up.

2. God's holiness is the infinite, unrivaled love that the Father, the Son, and the Holy Spirit have eternally shared and enjoyed. God's holiness is his perfection, beauty, and purity. He is uncontaminated by anything unclean, impure, or unjust. And he is perfectly unique, different, and other than all he has created.

3. Atonement reconciles and restores our relationship with God. Abba, who is slow to anger, filled with mercy unending, overflowing in compassion, and loving to his children, sent his Son to atone for our sins.

4. There is nothing like a heart that has encountered the holy beauty of God and has become regenerated, remade, redirected, and repurposed for God's mission.

CHAPTER 5

Our Father Is Yahweh

Daddy is a powerful word. At its best, the word describes the man you look to for love, affirmation, courage, and wisdom.

Growing up, I did not look forward to being a dad. I didn't look forward to getting married either. The first wedding I went to was my own.

I was so focused on escaping my childhood environment, playing college football, and making it to the NFL that being a husband and dad was low on my list of priorities. Like most people, I prepared to have a successful career, which meant status and money. I trained my mind and body to be a world-class athlete. But I had no training in the art of being a husband or a father.

On June 17, 1996, a beautiful, brown-eyed girl came into my life when our daughter, Presley, was born. When I found out that Vicki and I were expecting, I was hoping for a son. At about the six-month mark of our pregnancy, I had a vivid dream, where I could see Presley's face. Ever since that dream, I have loved Presley deeply. *Papi*, the name she affectionately started calling me when she was about three years old, marks how we love each other. On August 22, 2000, our son, Jeremiah, was born. We nicknamed him "Big Bull" because he has always been big.

Becoming a father was a mixture of happiness and fear.

"Would I screw my kids up?"

"Would I be able to protect them from our evil world?"

"Would I be someone they run to, or someone they run from?"

When Jeremiah was about three, he started having bad nightmares that would cause him to wake up crying. As his dad, I wanted to protect and comfort him. I wanted him to know that he was safe in my arms.

A friend of ours invited us to stay at his cabin in the North Carolina mountains. Vicki and I slept in the master bedroom while the kids slept in another room. Late one night, Jeremiah let out a terror-filled scream. Coming out of a deep sleep, I bounced out of my bed, sprinted to his room, and held him in my arms. I reassured him, "Daddy is here. I've got you, son." The sound of his cries compelled me to go into rescue mode. When my children cry, I hear them. I am on my way.

If this is true of me, it is enormously more true for our Abba. When we pray, "Our Father," we are not praying to a distant, uninvolved, abstract thing called "god." We are praying to the living God, our Father who "abound[s] in faithful love" (Ps. 86:15).

Our *Abba* is not a deadbeat dad.

He is near.

He is present.

His concern for us touches our biggest problems and smallest details.

He hears our cries before we ever speak a word.

**OUR *ABBA* IS NOT
A DEADBEAT DAD.**

"Even before they call, I will answer; while they are still speaking, I will hear." (Isa. 65:24)

Seduced, Deceived, and Redeemed

The children of Adam—that is, me, you, and everyone ever born except Jesus of Nazareth—were not meant to experience things that would cause us to cry out in need of rescuing. The Tree of Life provided us with all we needed (Gen. 2:9). As we ate from the Tree of Life, we shared in the life of God. We had perfect union and communion in the eternal love feast of the Father, the Son, and Spirit. We were safe in Abba's loving embrace. Adam and his offspring were fashioned by Divine Love himself to be loved, so we would multiply and fill the earth with God's glory, which is another way of saying his faithful love (Gen. 1:28).

For love to really be love, a choice must exist. Adam and Eve had the choice to love God in return, or not. Unfortunately, the Creator and his image-bearers would experience a divorce. As described in Genesis 3, the dark power, Satan, spawned an evil web of deception that caught Adam and Eve and their offspring in its death grip. Once the seducer convinced Adam and Eve that God could not be trusted, their choice was clear. They chose not to love God.

Then, hell was poured out on humanity and creation. We are not as we should be, and neither is the world. Death, decay, and destruction mark our lives now.

We need to be made right with God.

We need redemption.

Ever since the dark power seduced Adam and Eve in the garden of Eden, people have been enslaved to sin and death (Gen. 3:1–6). But this is not the real enemy. Sin and death are consequences of the real enemy—idolatry.

Idolatry is not a word that twenty-first-century people use much. It sounds old-fashioned. *The worship of idols.* But you probably don't have any idols in your house that you pray to or sing to or worship. That might be true of people centuries ago, or in different parts of the world, but not you and I, right?

Idolatry is simply replacing the uncreated Creator with created things and exchanging "the glory of the immortal God for images" (Rom. 1:23). Idolatry is when we set our affections on anything or anyone to give us ultimate love, value, and purpose. Whatever we look to for the ultimate things in life is our god, and anything besides the one true God is a false god. It might be money, sex, pleasure, body image, the opinions of others, politics, safety. Looking for satisfaction in these things is idolatry.

Like any seducer, forces of evil are skilled at turning a good thing into a god thing. When good things are worshiped as gods, idolatry distorts our humanity. Instead of imaging forth God's glory as we were created to, we are enslaved to idols and demonic powers that corrupt us at every level of our being.

Therefore, Abba says,

> "I am the Lord your God, who brought you out
> of the land of Egypt, out of the place of slavery.
> Do not have other gods besides me. Do not make
> an idol for yourself, whether in the shape of any-
> thing in the heavens above or on the earth below
> or in the waters under the earth. Do not bow in

worship to them, and do not serve them; for I, the LORD your God, am a jealous God." (Exod. 20:1–5)

It was Abba's grace that set his people free from slavery to their idols so they could worship him, take upon his love, his agenda, and his character. Abba is jealous in the sense that he knows that if we give our hearts to another, sin and death are the consequences. Jesus reaffirms this when he says,

> "The most important [command] is Listen, Israel! The Lord our God, the Lord is one. Love the Lord your God with all your heart, with all your soul, with all your mind, and with all your strength. The second is, Love your neighbor as yourself. There is no other command greater than these." (Mark 12:29–31)

The first four commandments are about loving God and the following six are about loving your neighbor (Exod. 20:1–17). We have been created to enjoy the love of Abba, to live in the love of Abba, and to give away the love of Abba. Our love for Abba flows from viewing the mercies of God. As we remember King Jesus' sinless life, atoning death on the cross, and his resurrection, the mercy of God captures us. Abba fights for our hearts. He fights with a cross and an empty tomb.

WE HAVE BEEN CREATED TO ENJOY THE LOVE OF ABBA, TO LIVE IN THE LOVE OF ABBA, AND TO GIVE AWAY THE LOVE OF ABBA.

As I grow as Jesus' apprentice, I discover more and more how idolatry strips us of our humanity. A person is truly made human by participating in the life of God, imaging forth the glory of the Creator. The garden of Eden was God's temple, where heaven and earth overlapped. When God breathed life into Adam and Eve, he created his first royal priests. The first family was to birth a kingdom of priests who had the sacred vocation of joyfully expressing Abba's wise, beautiful, and loving reign to all the earth. Humanity alive is Abba glorified.

When we choose idolatry, we are choosing to renounce our right to rule and reign with our Creator. We are born to reign with God; therefore, we need to be born again so we can enter our sacred purpose.

> If by the one man's trespass, death reigned through that one man, how much more will those who receive the overflow of grace and the gift of righteousness reign in life through the one man, Jesus Christ. (Rom. 5:17)

We don't like to talk about "sin" very much in our culture. Like idolatry, it sounds old school, like some mean old man is calling everyone a bunch of sinners. But perhaps we have the wrong view of sin.

Sin is bigger than "I did bad." It's not some failure to follow an arbitrary set of rules. Sin is choosing to dehumanize ourselves by worshiping something or someone that is not Abba. Yes, sin is an offense to God, but it harms us. Because of sin, instead of fulfilling our sacred purpose as a kingdom of priests who rule with their Creator, we are plummeted into a subhuman existence.

The consequences of our idolatry are great. But God's grace is greater.

> But where sin multiplied, grace multiplied even more so that, just as sin reigned in death, so also grace will reign through righteousness, resulting in eternal life through Jesus Christ our Lord. (Rom. 5:20–21)

Because of our failure to worship our Creator, who is the eternal source of love, life and purpose, the Jewish prophet Isaiah describes our condition as being like blind prisoners sitting in a dark dungeon (Isa. 42:6–7). Until our spiritual eyes are opened to see ourselves this way, we will see no need for Jesus. Abba sent Jesus to remedy our condition.

> "The Spirit of the Lord is on me,
> because he has anointed me
> to preach good news to the poor.
> He has sent me
> to proclaim release to the captives
> and recovery of sight to the blind,
> to set free the oppressed,
> to proclaim the year of the Lord's favor."
> (Luke 4:18–19)

Despite our waywardness, God was always on his way to rescue us. He heard our cries for help. Like a loving, protective daddy, he ran to us with open arms, an eternal redemption and covenant in hand, inviting us back into his family (Heb. 9:12–14).

DESPITE OUR WAYWARDNESS, GOD WAS ALWAYS ON HIS WAY TO RESCUE US.

Abba Keeps His Promise

Since the garden of Eden, the children of Adam have been running and hiding from Abba. Fortunately, Abba has been running to find us, forgive us, and restore us. Genesis 11 describes humanity wanting to be like a god as they constructed a tower to reach heaven. Therefore, in a gracious act of judgment, God scattered his people. Then in Genesis 12, God unfolded a plan to gather his kids back unto himself. He made a covenant, an unbreakable promise, with a man named Abraham (Gen. 12:1–3). Abba promises to give life, love, his presence, his power, and his purpose to the multiethnic family of Abram (Gal. 3:8, 28–29). By grace through faith, Abraham and his descendants would be the vehicle through which the world would come to know and love him as Abba.

Not all would be smooth going, however. As God was forming the family he promised Abraham through his descendant Joseph, circumstances would change for his people. Through a series of divinely directed events described in Genesis, Joseph was in Egypt and made critical decisions that saved the nation from starvation (50:20). As a result, Abraham's family had favor with Pharaoh who loved Joseph. However, time passed, Pharoah died, and as God's people multiplied, they became a threat to "a new king, who did not know about Joseph" (Exod. 1:8). The new Pharaoh, who would have seen himself as a god,[1] saw a slave labor force, not God's missionary force through whom he would save the world (Exod. 1:8–14).

The words *oppressed, ruthless, bitter,* and *difficult* describe the conditions of God's covenant people in slavery. Similarly, sin is a harsh master. It oppresses us, treats us ruthlessly, and makes our lives bitter and difficult. I suspect the hard conditions of slavery in Egypt caused God's people to doubt his promise.

The last few years have been hard for all of us. Maybe you doubt that Abba is faithful to keep his promises?

Take heart—God hears the cries of his enslaved people.

> After a long time, the king of Egypt died. The Israelites groaned because of their difficult labor, they cried out, and their cry for help because of the difficult labor ascended to God. God heard their groaning, and God remembered his covenant with Abraham, with Isaac, and with Jacob. God saw the Israelites, and God knew. (Exod. 2:23–25)

A Wise Mother, a Promise-Keeping Father

Abba will keep his promise. He kept it to the Israelites through a poor Hebrew mother named Jochebed, who loved her baby son. For three months, she hid him to save his life. Pharaoh had given an order that if a Hebrew woman had a male child, the child was to be

---

[1] James K. Hoffmeier, "Son of God: From Pharaoh to Israel's Kings to Jesus," https://www.baslibrary.org/bible-review/13/3/10 (accessed September 20, 2020).

killed to reduce the population of Israelites in his land: "If the child is a son, kill him, but if it's a daughter, she may live" (Exod. 1:16).

This gives us a glimpse into the intense oppression of God's people. They were growing and flourishing despite their slavery, and the evil Pharaoh was so paranoid—felt so threatened by their population growth—that he would go to wicked ends to stop it.

When she could no longer hide him, Jochebed placed the boy in a basket of reeds by the bank of the Nile. Then God used another woman, Miriam, the baby boy's sister, to keep watch over him from a distance until he could be discovered by someone who could protect him. One day, Pharaoh's daughter heard the baby crying and felt sorry for him.

God answers our cries through people—sometimes unexpected people.

> Then [Miriam] said to Pharaoh's daughter, "Should I go and call a Hebrew woman who is nursing to nurse the boy for you?"
>
> "Go," Pharaoh's daughter told her. So the girl went and called the boy's mother. Then Pharaoh's daughter said to her, "Take this child and nurse him for me, and I will pay your wages." So the woman took the boy and nursed him. When the child grew older, she brought him to Pharaoh's daughter, and he became her son. She named him Moses, "Because," she said, "I drew him out of the water." (Exod. 2:7–10)

God is so faithful to keep his covenant that Moses' own mother was able to nurse her baby and get paid for it. No matter how uncertain things are, time and time again, God is faithful to keep his covenant. No matter how tough our enemies are, God can even use them to bless us.

NO MATTER HOW UNCERTAIN THINGS ARE, TIME AND TIME AGAIN, GOD IS FAITHFUL TO KEEP HIS COVENANT.

Bush on Fire

As Moses grew, he was a Hebrew raised with the privilege of Egyptian royalty. He knew the sufferings of the oppressed and the power of the oppressor. Watching his people hurt but living in the comfort of his position, his soul was being torn apart.

Power and privilege are hard to give up when they grant us pleasure. But justice requires that we share our power and privilege and get uncomfortable, so that the oppressed and powerless can experience freedom. This submission is what Jesus did by coming to earth to save us (Phil. 2:3–11).

One day, while Moses was out among his people, the Hebrews, he saw an Egyptian taskmaster beating one of them. In a desire to enact justice, Moses killed him and buried him in the sand.

Marinate on this: first, *justice without Jesus is vengeance.* God's mercy is for the oppressor *and* the oppressed. Repentance of the oppressor, forgiveness from the oppressed, reconciliation of the enemies with human flourishing—these things are God's heart.

JUSTICE WITHOUT JESUS
IS VENGEANCE.

Second, *we cannot bury our sins in the sand and think no one will know.* God knows and sees all. We must bury our sins in Jesus. Only he can bury them so Abba "will never again remember [our] sins and [our] lawless acts" (Heb. 10:17).

Moses is found out.

The people attempt to kill him.

Moses flees to the land of Midian.

For the next forty years in exile, Abba shapes Moses into his means of keeping his covenant with Abraham. Moses is emptied, so God can fill Moses with himself.

Humility prepares us to receive new abilities and callings from God. As God molds Moses like a potter molds clay, his covenant people are crying out for help, and God is getting ready to use Moses (Exod. 2:23–25).

Did you know that you, too, are the answer to someone's cries for help? God's redemption is carried from person-to-person like a holy, life-giving virus.

After forty long years in exile due to his crime, Moses encountered God in a burning bush (Exod. 3:2). Often in the Old Testament when the "Angel of the Lord" appears, it is the presence of God on earth, called a Christophany.[2] A Christophany is the appearance of the preincarnate Christ in the Old Testament.

In this Christophany, God told Moses that he had observed the misery of the Hebrew people because of their oppression. He was

---

[2] See Genesis 16:7–13; 21:17–21; 31:10–13; Judges 2:1.

coming to liberate them. He was coming to keep his promise (Exod. 3:7–8). I suspect Moses was excited until God said,

> Because the Israelites' cry for help has come to me, and I have also seen the way the Egyptians are oppressing them, therefore, go. I am sending you to Pharaoh so that you may lead my people, the Israelites, out of Egypt." (Exod. 3:9–10)

God is going to rescue his children, but he is going to do the rescuing through Moses. Before Moses reluctantly agreed to go to Pharaoh on behalf of God, he said,

> "If I go to the Israelites and say to them, 'The God of your ancestors has sent me to you,' and they ask me, 'What is his name?' what should I tell them?"
> God replied to Moses, "I AM WHO I AM. This is what you are to say to the Israelites: I AM has sent me to you." God also said to Moses, "Say this to the Israelites: The LORD, the God of your ancestors, the God of Abraham, the God of Isaac, and the God of Jacob, has sent me to you. This is my name forever; this is how I am to be remembered in every generation." (Exod. 3:13–15)

Abba reveals himself as *ehyeh 'ašer 'ehyeh*. This phrase translates to "I AM WHO I AM" or "I will be who I will be." Scholars call this the *tetragrammaton*, which is the four letters YHWH. They translate this as *ehyeh* or *Yahweh*. In English, the word *Jehovah* is sometimes used for Yahweh. The sacred name of Abba reveals that he is the eternal, self-existent, self-determining One. He is present with his people and is faithful to keep his covenant to his people because he loves us.

When we pray "Our Father," we are praying to the great I AM.

I AM present with you in your struggle.

I AM going to deliver you from slavery.

I AM going to father you.

Through Moses, the Great I AM is victorious over the ten false gods of the Egyptians, forcing Pharaoh to let his kids go free (Exod. 7:14–Exod. 13).

One Greater Than Moses

One greater than Moses also came to free God's people from the greater Pharaoh of sin and death (Heb. 3:3–4). Just as Abba sent Moses to lead his people out of the chains of slavery, he also sent his eternal Son, who himself is the great I AM, to lead his people out of the chains of sin and idolatry:

> Jesus said to them, "Truly I tell you, before Abraham was, I am." (John 8:58)

This greater Moses, who is the great I AM in human form, is also the greater "Passover lamb" and "the guarantee of a better covenant" (1 Cor. 5:7; Heb. 7:22). In Messiah Jesus, Abba's covenant promise is fulfilled. Through the sinless life of Jesus, his sacrificial death on the cross, and his resurrection, all who trust in him are regenerated, redeemed, reconciled, and restored into the family God promised Abraham.

And if you belong to Christ, then you are Abraham's seed, heirs according to the promise. (Gal. 3:29)

THROUGH THE SINLESS LIFE OF JESUS, HIS SACRIFICIAL DEATH ON THE CROSS, AND HIS RESURRECTION, ALL WHO TRUST IN HIM ARE REGENERATED, REDEEMED, RECONCILED, AND RESTORED INTO THE FAMILY GOD PROMISED ABRAHAM.

We are journeying on a new exodus to the greater promised land called the new heavens and new earth, where we will dwell in resurrected, glorified bodies with our God, ruling and reigning at his side.

Abba hears our cries.

Jesus is Abba's response to our cries for help. He is Abba's "Yes, I have heard you, and I AM faithful to my promise."

For every one of God's promises is "Yes" in him. Therefore, through him we also say "Amen" to the glory of God. Now it is God who strengthens us together with you in Christ, and who has anointed us. He has also put his seal on us and given us the Spirit in our hearts as a down payment. (2 Cor. 1:20–22)

—————————— Marinate on This ——————————

Prayer

Abba,

You are faithful in all your ways.

You are the God of Abraham, Isaac, and Jacob.

Before I ever cried out for help

You were on your way.

Before I knew I needed your grace

You provided a way to bring my heart to yours.

You are the Great I AM.

Burn in me the way you burned in that bush.

The shackles of sin and death have been forever broken.

Thank you for loving me, guiding me, and inviting
me into the family you promised Abraham.

"And if you belong to Christ, then you are Abraham's
seed, heirs according to the promise" (Gal. 3:29).

In Jesus' name, amen.

Questions to Reflect On

1. Is it natural for you to think of God as your Father, or is it difficult? Why?

2. What did you learn in this chapter about the story of humanity and our need for salvation?

3. What did the story of YHWH freeing his people from slavery teach you about God's character?

4. Has this chapter made you want to pray more? Has it made God seem more beautiful and glorious to you? If so, how?

Things to Remember

1. We have been created to enjoy the love of Abba, to live in the love of Abba, and to give away the love of Abba.

2. Since the garden of Eden, the children of Adam have been running and hiding from Abba. Fortunately, Abba has been running to find us, forgive us, and restore us.

3. No matter how uncertain things are, time and time again, God is faithful to keep his covenant.

4. Through the sinless life of Jesus, his sacrificial death on the cross, and his resurrection, all who trust in him are regenerated, redeemed, reconciled, and restored into the family God promised Abraham.

CHAPTER 6

Our Father Is Good

November 9, 2018, was a chilly North Carolina evening, but you could feel the warmth of excitement in your bones.

Overflow crowds were standing on the track and up the hills behind the benches of each football team. Horns were blaring. Cattle bells were ringing. People were yelling. Cheerleaders were chanting.

My son's high school football team was playing in their second consecutive state championship. As a junior, he had experienced winning a state championship. And now, as one of the senior captains on the team, he had the opportunity to win back-to-back state titles.

I was happy for Jeremiah. This moment was the culmination of years of hard work. As the son of a former NFL player, people will mistakenly think that it was easy for him. It was not. In middle school until his sophomore year, he grew so fast that it took time for his mind and body to get on the same page. Nevertheless, his work ethic, his attention to detail, and his desire to honor what he was doing were always present.

By the time Jeremiah was a senior in high school, he stood 6'1", weighed 210, ran a 4.5 forty-meter dash, and had a 36" vertical leap. As a high school senior, he was taller, bigger, and faster than I was as an NFL player! Jeremiah was one of the top high school football players in America, with multiple football scholarship offers. His focus, execution, and athleticism were those of a true craftsman. When people watched Jeremiah, they saw a marvelous athlete with incredible talent. But I saw my son, who worked harder than anyone I had ever been around.

The state championship game was going according to plan. Jeremiah and his defensive teammates were playing smart, fast, and physical. But then it happened. The whistle blew. The play was over. The players from both teams got up off the ground and went back to their huddles. But Jeremiah did not.

He was still on the ground.

His teammates waved at the coaches and medical staff to come to the field. They gathered around Jeremiah, and I could tell he was badly hurt. I knew because he clutched the pant leg of one of the medical staff. That is exactly what I did when I broke my leg and tore ligaments in my knee in 1998 against the Dallas Cowboys.

Time slowed down.

My heart began to beat out of my chest.

Fear was present.

The coach signaled for me, and I ran to the field and broke through the circle of coaches and medical staff surrounding my son. I got down on one knee and put my left hand on his chest. With my right, I instinctively started to stroke his head. Jeremiah had a tear making its way down his left cheek. I looked at him and smiled. I said, "Son, I love you. I am so proud of you. You literally gave it all so your team could win."

The medical staff carried him off the field and placed him on the bench. His ankle was about three times its normal size. The lower part of his leg was broken in eight different places and several ankle ligaments were ruptured. Jeremiah sustained a significant injury. It was bad. But something happened in that moment that has transformed our lives forever.

Even though the stadium was bursting with loud people, Jeremiah and I had a moment where all I could hear was him. On the inside, my heart was being torn apart. I was hurting for my son.

He was badly injured.

He was missing the state championship game with his brothers.

He was facing surgery and a long rehab.

In this moment, Jeremiah looked at me with the biggest smile on his face, and he said, "Dad, God is so good."

I said, "What did you say, son?"

He said, "Dad, God is so good."

I said, "Son, why do you say that?"

He said, "Dad, I could have been hurt in the first game of the season. I could have been hurt really bad." In my mind, I am thinking, *Son, do you have any idea how big your ankle is right now?*

But with the biggest, most peaceful smile—despite a broken leg and ruptured ankle ligaments—my eighteen-year-old son was praising God for his goodness. He was not praising God because he made the biggest play to help his team win. He was not praising God because he played the best game of his life. He was praising God when it made no sense to praise him. The depths of God's goodness met him. My heart of trepidation transformed into a heart of praise. I started praising the goodness of God too!

Jeremiah's team won, but he got something so much more valuable than a ring. The goodness of Abba got him. Even during pain and disappointment, he tasted and saw that Abba was good.

> Taste and see that the LORD is good. How happy
> is the person who takes refuge in him! (Ps. 34:8)

When you pray, "Our Father," you are praying to our good, good Abba.

Abba Is Good

The goodness of Abba describes his essential nature that overflows in love and kindness toward his kids. Abba is tenderhearted, full of sympathy, and unfailing in his commitment to keep his redemptive promises.

God is good . . . all the time.

Abba's goodness is eternal, unchanging, and uncaused.

You can trust him.

He is for you.

If you ever do doubt Abba is for you, look to the cross and the empty tomb.

 ABBA'S GOODNESS IS ETERNAL, UNCHANGING, AND UNCAUSED.

> But God proves his own love for us in that while we were still sinners, Christ died for us. (Rom 5:8)

> What, then, are we to say about these things? If God is for us, who is against us? He did not even spare his own Son but gave him up for us all. How will he not also with him grant us everything? (Rom. 8:31–32)

The "everything" that Abba will give his kids is that he is sovereignly working all things—the good, the bad, and the unexplainable—to form us into the image of Jesus (Rom. 8:28–29). He is a refuge in the storms of life and a hiding place of grace where we are safe:

> How great is the goodness you have stored up for those who fear you. You lavish it on those who come to you for protection, blessing them before the watching world. (Ps. 31:19 NLT)

The goodness of Abba is the catalyst behind his passion to bless us. He is so good that even people who have chosen to not follow his Son Jesus benefit from his goodness.

> "He never left them without evidence of himself and his goodness. For instance, he sends you rain and good crops and gives you food and joyful hearts." (Acts 14:17 NLT)

This goodness is also the impetus behind his passion to redeem all of humanity and creation itself (Rom. 8:22–24).

> Every good and perfect gift is from above, coming down from the Father of lights, who does not change like shifting shadows. By his own choice, he gave us birth by the word of truth so that we would be a kind of firstfruits of his creatures. (James 1:17–18)

It is the goodness of Abba that sent Jesus to the cross.
It is the goodness of Abba that raised Jesus from the dead.

It is the goodness of Abba that gave us a new birth and filled us with infinite worth.

It is the goodness of Abba that calls you a loved, accepted, forgiven, pure, clean, and holy child.

It is the goodness of Abba that convicts you of your sin when you are off the path of life.

It is the goodness of Abba that whispers, "You are loved. Do not do it. I have plans for you," when you were thinking about killing yourself.

It is the goodness of Abba that reminds you, "I will never leave you or forsake you," when your spouse abandons you for another.

It is the goodness of Abba that watches your dreams end and carries you in the midst of them to recognize his blessings.

It is the goodness of Abba that will take your worst pain and give your life its greatest purpose.

God's Name Reflects His Character

Often parents name their children in hopes that they will embody the meaning of the name they were given. At our first birth, our biological parents named us. My parents named me Derwin Lamont Gray. Derwin means "dear friend," and Lamont means "mountain." My name means "dear friend who is like a mountain." At our second birth, when we came through a womb called Jesus' tomb, Abba gives us a name also. Our new name is cherished, holy, perfect, and blood-bought. He also calls us the body of Christ and royal priests. Through the wonderful mystery called grace, these names are given to us as pure gifts (Eph. 2:8–9). These names, through the Spirit's presence, call us to become who Abba already declares us to be.

Just as our second birth gives us names that describe who we are in Christ, and who we will become through Christ, Abba has names that shout from the rooftops his goodness. Here are a few of his names.

God Is Yahweh-Shalom

He is our peace. Our peace is not found in circumstances, but in Abba himself, as Jesus, the Prince of Peace, inhabits our being through the Holy Spirit.

> But the LORD said to him, "Peace to you. Don't be afraid, for you will not die." So Gideon built an altar to the LORD there and called it The LORD Is Peace. (Judg. 6:23–24)

God Is Yahweh-Rapha

He is our healer. In Abba's grace, through his crucified and risen Son, via the Spirit's power, our scars become testimonies of his goodness.

> The Spirit of the Lord GOD is on me, because the LORD has anointed me to bring good news to the poor. He has sent me to heal the brokenhearted, to proclaim liberty to the captives and freedom to the prisoners. (Isa. 61:1)

God Is Yahweh-Tsabbaoth

He is the *Lord of Hosts*, which means he is the Lord Almighty. Abba, in a beautiful symphony, with his eternal Son and the Spirit, sovereignly orchestrates and reigns over his creation. Ultimately through Messiah Jesus, he directs all of creation toward its intended redemptive purposes, the new heavens and new earth.

> And one called to another: "Holy, holy, holy is the LORD of Armies; his glory fills the whole earth." (Isa. 6:3)

> And this is the plan: At the right time he will bring everything together under the authority of Christ—everything in heaven and on earth. Furthermore, because we are united with Christ, we have received an inheritance from God, for he chose us in advance, and he makes everything work out according to his plan. (Eph. 1:10–11 NLT)

God Is Yahweh-Yireh

He is our provider. Abba may not always give us what we want, but he will always give us what we need. Every need is met in Christ and extended to us by the Spirit (Phil. 4:19).

> But the angel of the LORD called to him from heaven and said, "Abraham, Abraham!" He replied, "Here I am." Then he said, "Do not lay a hand on the boy or do anything to him. For now I know that you fear God, since you have not withheld your only son from me." Abraham looked up and saw a ram caught in the thicket by its horns. So Abraham went and took the ram and offered it as a burnt offering in place of his son. And Abraham named that place The LORD Will Provide, so today it is said, "It will be provided on the LORD's mountain." (Gen. 22:11–14)

God Is Yahweh-Tsidkenu

He is our righteousness. In an act of grace, Abba calls us to share life in union with Jesus, by the Holy Spirit's power. We are swept up into Abba's righteousness in Christ, so we can be reconciled to him and each other, and so we can embody his righteousness on the earth.

> In his days Judah will be saved, and Israel will dwell securely. This is the name he will be called: The LORD Is Our Righteousness. (Jer. 23:6)

> He made the one who did not know sin to be sin for us, so that in him we might become the righteousness of God. (2 Cor. 5:21)

God Is Yahweh-Shammah

He "is there," wherever there is. King David affirms the hope-giving reality that the *thereness* of Abba is perpetually present with us: "Where can I go to escape your Spirit? Where can I flee from your presence?" (Ps. 139:7). Abba in Messiah Jesus, through the Spirit, is a circle whose center is everywhere and whose circumference is nowhere.[1] Nothing or no one has ever moved without him seeing it. There is not a secret motive that he does not know.

> Distance cannot keep him away from us.

> Darkness cannot elude his light.

> Death cannot escape his life.

---

[1] Adrian Rogers, "The Names of God in the Bible"; cited in https://www.lwf.org/names-of-god, September 29, 2020.

His thereness is wherever there is.

When we are discouraged, his thereness encourages us through the dark valley.

When we are lonely, his thereness befriends us.

When we are worried, his thereness calms our anxious hearts.

When we are tempted, his thereness is our way of escape.[2]

"Am I a God who is only near"—this is the LORD's declaration—"and not a God who is far away? Can a person hide in secret places where I cannot see him?"—the LORD's declaration. "Do I not fill the heavens and the earth?"—the LORD's declaration. (Jer. 23:23–24)

God Is Yahweh-Nissi

He is our banner. This means that as Abba's kids, we are covered by his sovereign goodness, no matter the circumstance, we have the "overwhelming victory" through King Jesus, who loves us (Rom. 8:37 NLT). The ultimate sign of God's victory is Jesus' life, death, and resurrection. This is Abba's banner of victory that he waves over us in the midst of the battle.

And Moses built an altar and named it, "The LORD Is My Banner." (Exod. 17:15)

---

[2] Rogers, "The Names of God in the Bible."

THE ULTIMATE SIGN OF GOD'S VICTORY IS JESUS' LIFE, DEATH, AND RESURRECTION.

God Is Yahweh-Raah

He is our shepherd. The goodness of Abba is explained in the metaphor of being a shepherd who knows and loves his sheep. The perfect picture of Abba is showcased in his incarnate, eternal Son, King Jesus, who is the Great Shepherd.

> Now may the God of peace, who brought up from the dead our Lord Jesus—the great Shepherd of the sheep—through the blood of the everlasting covenant, equip you with everything good to do his will, working in us what is pleasing in his sight, through Jesus Christ, to whom be glory forever and ever. Amen. (Heb. 13:20–21)

Tucked away in the splendor of Psalm 23, hiding in plain sight, is each of these Old Testament names of God.[3]

I was walking through some challenging things a few year ago. I had to make some difficult leadership decisions at Transformation Church. There was some pain from my past resurfacing and thrashing in my mind. I was really hurting. But God in his grace led me to marinate on Psalm 23. Abba, our Shepherd, met me and ministered to me. *My problems were not fixed, but I learned to fix my eyes on him.* Just about every night for the last five

---

[3] Warren W. Wiersbe, *Wiersbe's Expository Outlines on the Old Testament* (Ps 22–24) (Wheaton, IL: Victor Books, 1993), 441.

years, by memory, I have slowly quoted Psalm 23. I pray it over me, my family, Transformation Church, and the worldwide Church. I pray especially, that we would be a people that incarnate Psalm 23. Psalm 23 is a prayer that explored that goodness of God. Notice how the names of God are reflected in each verse:

> *Yahweh-Raah,* "The Lord is our shepherd."
> The LORD is my shepherd (v. 1a)
>
> *Yahweh-Jireh,* "The Lord will provide."
> I have what I need. (v. 1b)
>
> *Yahweh-Shalom,* "The Lord is our peace."
> He lets me lie down in green pastures; he leads
> me beside quiet waters. (v. 2)
>
> *Yahweh-Rapha,* "The Lord will heal."
> He renews my life. (v. 3a)
>
> *Yahweh-Tsidkenu,* "The Lord is our righteousness."
> He leads me along the right paths for his name's
> sake. (v. 3b)
>
> *Yahweh-Shammah,* "The Lord is there."
> Even when I go through the darkest valley, I fear
> no danger, for you are with me; your rod and
> your staff—they comfort me. (v. 4)
>
> *Yahweh-Nissi,* "The Lord is our banner."
> You prepare a table before me in the presence of
> my enemies; you anoint my head with oil; my
> cup overflows. Only goodness and faithful love

will pursue me all the days of my life, and I will
dwell in the house of the LORD as long as I live.
(vv. 5–6)

Holy Is Your Name

Our Abba hears us.

He is a good, good father.

Therefore, we treat his name as holy. There is no one like him.
He has earned our allegiance because of his epic acts of grace. When
Jesus teaches us to pray, "Therefore, you should pray like this: 'Our
Father in heaven, your name be honored as holy'" (Matt. 6:9), we
are joining Jesus in using "Abba" as a substitute for the Divine
Name, Yahweh (I AM).[4] Yahweh is good. And when we call him
Abba, we are declaring our allegiance to the One who is worthy of
adoration. He alone is able to redeem us. No other name will do
(Acts 4:12). There is no other Name by which humanity and cre-
ation can be redeemed.

Our Father in Heaven

When we pray, "Our Father in heaven," we are doing so much
more than just asking for stuff. We are entering into the very heart
of God. We are diving deeper into his character, his redemptive
story, his love, and his sacred purpose.

God wants us to know him. Yahweh is loving, sovereign, holy,
and good. It is impossible to trust someone you do not know. And

---

[4] Richard Bauckham, *Who Is God?* (Grand Rapids: Baker Academic,
2020), 55.

when we get to know him, through his Son and by the Spirit, our allegiance to him becomes a joyful act of worship. As we pray "Our Father," his story becomes our story. We experience his covenantal faithfulness to create a loving, beautifully diverse family in his Son. As we pray "Our Father," we discover that the most important thing in life is to leverage our lives so others can experience Abba's love in Christ Jesus.

 GOD WANTS US TO KNOW HIM.

> For the love of Christ compels us, since we have reached this conclusion, that one died for all, and therefore all died. And he died for all so that those who live should no longer live for themselves, but for the one who died for them and was raised. (2 Cor. 5:14–15)

─────────────── Marinate on This ───────────────

Prayer

Abba,

You are good.

Goodness is who you are.

Even when I cannot see it

Give me the grace to believe it.

You are good

And all the time you are good.

Abba,

Your goodness is uncaused

But it is the cause of every good and perfect gift.

Abba,

Your goodness sent Jesus to the cross.

Your goodness raised Jesus from the dead.

Your goodness gave us a new birth and
filled us with infinite worth.

Abba,

Your goodness takes our worst pain and gives
our lives their greatest purposes.

God, do you hear me?

You are good. And all the time you are good.

In Jesus' name, amen.

Questions for Reflection

1. Why is it so hard to affirm that God is good when you are in a hard situation or season of life?

2. How can we know, without any shadow of a doubt, that God is good?

3. Which of the names of God stood out to you, and why?

4. How should the goodness of God inform our prayer life?

Things to Remember

1. The goodness of Abba describes his essential nature that overflows in love and kindness toward his kids. Abba is tenderhearted, full of sympathy, and unfailing in his commitment to keep his redemptive promises.

2. It is the goodness of Abba that will take your worst pain and give your life its greatest purpose.

3. The perfect picture of Abba is showcased in his incarnate, eternal Son, King Jesus, who is the Great Shepherd.

4. As we pray "Our Father," we discover that the most important thing in life is to leverage our lives so others can experience Abba's love in Christ Jesus.

Discovering God's Kingdom and Your Priestly Role in It

*"Your kingdom come. Your will be done
on earth as it is in heaven."*
MATTHEW 6:10

The better we know and understand Abba's kingdom and our priestly role in it, the more purposeful and fulfilling our life of prayer will be. As we walk through this section we will discover what it means to:

- Participate in the kingdom
- Proclaim the kingdom
- Personify the kingdom
- Pursue the kingdom

Prayer is not making stuff up as we go along. Prayer is us reminding ourselves of what Abba has already accomplished in and through Jesus. Jesus is what the kingdom of God looks like in bodily form and our priestly role in God's kingdom is to be formed into the image of Jesus. Prayer is rehearsing God's story and how we fit in his story for his glory.

CHAPTER 7

Participating in Abba's Kingdom

I want to tell you a story about a wise, good, and loving king. The king I speak of is different than all other kings. All other kings have a root of selfish ambition. They take from their citizens. This king gives gifts to his. All other kings are hungry for power. This king is hungry to serve the powerless. All other kings ask the citizens to fight their wars. This king fights wars on behalf of his citizens.

The king I speak of is different. He is the true king.

Imagine a king with unlimited power and limitless, life-giving, creative genius. Now, imagine that this king is eternal love himself. He has no needs because he is all-sufficient. In his wise goodness, he freely creates a universe to be his playground. And on the third rock from the sun, in a garden, he creates a temple.

In his garden temple, let us call it "The Place of Delight," he situates a man and woman. The man and woman will be priests, which means that they serve the king and reflect his glory on the earth. They also bear the king's image, which means they, too, are royalty. Because the king is wise and good, he promises to be with them and to provide for their every need. His life, which is the life from which all life originates, will be their source of life-giving love.

As the king's royal priests, the man and woman are given a sacred purpose. Their sacred purpose is to fill the earth with other image-bearers, so the king's wise and good rule can be displayed in and through them on earth. For his royal priests to truly love him and fulfill their sacred purposes, the king has to give them the ability to choose or reject his purpose for their lives.

In one day, all other days changed because the man and woman decided to reject and betray the good king.

Despite his loyal love, his hand of protection, his heart of provision, and his gracious presence, they leave his kingdom of light and walk into the kingdom of darkness. They think the king's creation is better than the king himself.

Instead of life, there is now death.

Instead of peace, there is now violence.

Instead of love, there is now sin—all sorts of sin.

An invasive dark power covers the land and poisons the image-bearers' hearts. Like DNA, the sin sickness of the original man and woman is passed into the genes of all their descendants.

LIKE DNA, THE SIN SICKNESS OF THE ORIGINAL MAN AND WOMAN IS PASSED INTO THE GENES OF ALL THEIR DESCENDANTS.

But the king, who had seen every possible outcome to every possible decision his children would make, had already decided before time began to restore his kingdom on earth and rescue his image-bearers. Despite the man and woman's uprising, the king would raise up a man named "The Father of Many." The king promised "The Father of Many" that his little nomadic tribe one day would be a big, single tribe of all the peoples on the earth. It would be a multicolored, multicultural tribe governed by the king.

This single, big family would start with a little, unimpressive tribe. The king set his affections on this little tribe. They were the apple of his eye. But not because of anything impressive in and of themselves. In fact, there was nothing impressive about them at all. They didn't add anything to the king. He simply chose to set his affections on them. He loved them, you might say, because he loved them.

This tribe was supposed to act as priests, just like the original man and woman. To accomplish their priestly purpose, the king would give them a unique way to live that would separate them from the other nations who had false kings. His presence would dwell among them. He would teach them how to love the king, themselves, and their neighbors. They would be a light in a world of darkness, and their light was to draw the people to its source— their king.

Through slavery in foreign lands under bad kings, the true king would not forsake them. He would rescue them. Through their disobedience, he would not abandon them. The king kept his promise to "The Father of Many." Ultimately, the little tribe, who constantly wrestled with the king, had their story completed in a surprising way. The king sent his own son to restore and establish his kingdom on earth.

THE KING SENT HIS OWN SON TO RESTORE AND ESTABLISH HIS KINGDOM ON EARTH.

The king's son shared authority with his father so much so that he is called the "King of kings." The king's son came and lived among the people. They beheld the king's glory in the face of the son. Many said, "To see the son is to see the father."

The king's son was sent on a mission to reconcile, reclaim, and restore his father's kingdom and his father's royal priests. But the sickness of the original image-bearers locked humanity in a dark dungeon of captivity. They were helpless and hopeless. On their own, freedom was impossible. The rescuing son-king came to heal the sin-sickness and free the captives. The saving son-king was the only one who could set the captives free and heal the sickness.

Because the son was a king, the essence of the true king, many thought he would use violence to set the captives free. Instead, the son-king allowed violence to overtake him so he could defeat sin and death. The son-king exchanged his life for the rebellious, sin-sick image-bearers' lives. This exchange was so great that all that was true of the son-king became true of all those who followed him.

The cost of acceptance was a perfect life. The son-king lived a perfect life.

The cost of freedom was blood. The son-king spilled his blood.

The cost of forgiveness was death. The son-king died.

But he did not stay dead.

Behind the original man and woman, committing treason against the king and dooming their offspring, were the dark forces. The dark forces thought the son-king would stay dead. For three days, he did. But early on a Sunday, the son-king rose before the sun did. And just like the brightness that comes from the sun, the son-king brought true light to the world.

Victory won.

Dark forces lost.

Sin-sickness was cured.

Death was swallowed up in eternal life.

Eventually, the son-king returned to his father, who dwelt in another realm. But he did not leave his followers alone. Image-bearers who pledge their allegiance to the son-king enter his kingdom. They become students of the son-king, growing up and *glowing up* to imitate his life as they learn to trust and draw life from his Spirit. The son-king informs his students that in their world there will be trouble, but they can still have courage, because he overcame the world and will one day remake it. Just like the son-king rose from the dead, all of creation will rise to newness.

Until that time, the family of royal priests is to give glimpses of the king's kingdom by fulfilling their royal purposes. The recreated people of the son-king are to dispense wisdom by acting justly, living faithfully, walking humbly with the king, and inviting others to join the son-king's kingdom. They are to let the light of the son-king shine through them so the whole earth will be filled with his glory.

Then one day, when it is least expected, the son-king will return to establish his kingdom on earth in all its fullness. The son-king's followers will rule and reign with him as coheirs, exploring the glories of God's creative genius. A new, indescribable, eternal adventure will ensue.

The king will return to dwell among his people.

The dark powers will be forever doomed, no longer a threat.

Those who choose to give their allegiance to false kings sadly will remain in darkness.

The Kingdom Story

We all love a good story. We are hardwired for them. I wrote the story above so it could echo in your soul and remind you of the ancient story of God's kingdom. God's kingdom story is the one you were made for.

Our world is filled with stories, all fiercely competing for our loyalty.

Politics tells a story.

Corporations tell a story.

Pornography tells a story.

Dysfunctional families tell a story.

Entertainment tells a story.

There are lots of stories. But there is one story, above all of the others, and it is the kingdom story. It is the genuine story that our hearts long for, and the one Abba invites us to participate in.

When we pray "your kingdom come . . . on earth as it is in heaven," we are requesting that our lives align with Abba's kingdom story. Prayer is not about getting what we want, as though we are spoiled six-year-olds pestering our mom for more Legos or dolls.

Prayer is about *participating* in Abba's kingdom story.

Prayer is about *proclaiming* Abba's kingdom story.

Prayer is about *personifying* Abba's kingdom story.

Prayer is about *pursuing* Abba's kingdom story.

You are called to participate in Abba's kingdom story, which goes like this:[1]

- Abba alone is King.
- Abba is now ruling in King Jesus.
- The Church, or Abba's kids, is now a family
  of Jews and Gentiles that are incorporated

---

[1] Scot McKnight, *Kingdom Conspiracy* (Grand Rapids: Brazos Press, 2014), 34.

into King Jesus and governed by his gracious
rule.

- Freedom from sin and death, along with
forgiveness from sin, is granted through King
Jesus.
- Abba's rule in King Jesus will be made complete in his future, final kingdom on earth
where Abba's kids will rule and reign with
Jesus.

What Is the Kingdom of God?

The kingdom of God means that Abba is invading the earth
with love, to challenge and correct the corrupted rule of human
kings that are under the influence of dark powers.[2] In Messiah
Jesus, Abba is now ruling, and his kingdom rule is redeeming,
regenerating, rescuing, justifying, reconciling, and transforming
people to bear a resemblance to Jesus on the earth.[3] This divine
invasion is what it means to pray and request God's kingdom to
come to earth.

When Jesus began his public ministry, he was participating in
the kingdom story. In ancient Israel, a prophet named John baptized
people in the Jordan River. Jesus left Galilee and met John at the
Jordan, so John could baptize him, too.

> But John tried to stop him, saying, "I need to be
> baptized by you, and yet you come to me?" Jesus
> answered him, "Allow it for now, because this is

---

[2] McKnight, 34.
[3] McKnight, 35.

the way for us to fulfill all righteousness." Then
John allowed him to be baptized. (Matt. 3:14–15)

Jesus, who had no sin, was baptized to identify with Israel,
humanity, and the kingdom of God. Jesus fulfills the righteousness
that Adam, Eve, and Israel could not. Jesus embodies the righteousness that the kingdom of God requires. When the Holy Spirit
awakens us to faith in Jesus, Jesus shares his righteousness with us.

This righteousness is given through faith in Jesus
Christ to all who believe. (Rom. 3:22 NIV)

When Jesus emerged from the Jordan River, the Spirit of God
descended on him like a dove. Abba spoke these words over his son,
"You are my beloved Son; with you I am well-pleased" (Mark 1:11).
Immediately following his baptism, God the Holy Spirit led Jesus
into the wilderness to be tempted by Satan (Matt. 4:1–11; Mark
1:12–13). In being baptized and enduring Satan's temptation in the
wilderness, Jesus was reenacting the story of Israel, a part of the
larger kingdom story.

There are multiple ways that Jesus identifies with Israel at this
moment. First, Jesus was baptized by entering the water just as the
people of Israel entered the water of the Red Sea when they were
escaping Pharaoh in the exodus. Also, in the wilderness after leaving Egypt, Israel was tempted three times by Satan and failed three
times (Deut. 8:3; 6:16; 6:13). In the wilderness, Jesus is tempted
three times by Satan but remains obedient (Matt. 4:1–11). Other
similarities are revealed in the mirroring of forty years in the wilderness by Israel and forty days by Jesus.

After Jesus left the wilderness and John was arrested by the
rulers, Jesus proclaimed, "The time is fulfilled, and the kingdom

of God has come near. Repent and believe the good news!" (Mark 1:15). *Repent* means to turn away from false kings and false stories and run to the true king and his story. The "good news" means that Abba sent Jesus, the new king, to redeem, reconcile, and regenerate a righteous family of royal priests, who exist to embody the kingdom of God in fulfillment with Abba's covenant with Abraham (Gal. 3:8).

The kingdom has come near because Jesus is the kingdom of God. So, what does the kingdom of God look like?

It looks like Jesus, and the way he lived and loved.

The way he healed and cried.

The way he washed his disciples' dirty feet.

The way he broke down racial and gender barriers to transform a Samaritan woman's life.

The way he was a friend to sinners like us.

The way he cleansed the temple of corrupt money changers.

The way he took the forgotten and made them known.

The way he left the ninety-nine to find the one.

The way he died.

The way he rose from the dead.

The way he will come again.

Jesus is the kingdom of God on full display.

When we pray "your kingdom come . . . on earth as it is in heaven," we are praying to participate in the kingdom story so we can become like the king of the story. His ways, his life, his attitude become ours (Phil. 2:5).

The Lord's Prayer *explains* the life Jesus lived on earth. Jesus is the kingdom of God. When you pray the Lord's Prayer, you are praying to *know* the king, to enter and *participate* in the kingdom, and to be *transformed* into the image of the king. Prayer is so much more than getting. Often, we pray for trinkets, but Abba wants to give us his Son.

WHEN YOU PRAY THE LORD'S PRAYER, YOU ARE PRAYING TO *KNOW* THE KING, TO ENTER AND *PARTICIPATE* IN THE KINGDOM, AND TO BE *TRANSFORMED* INTO THE IMAGE OF THE KING.

> He has rescued us from the domain of darkness and transferred us into the kingdom of the Son he loves. In him we have redemption, the forgiveness of sins. (Col. 1:13–14)

As Abba transfers us into his Son's kingdom, we are also transferred into real hope. Hope is not a strategy, a clever marketing plan, or a wish dream, but a person.

Kingdom Hope

In the Star Wars movie *The Last Jedi*, Princess Leia said, "Hope is like the sun. If you only believe it when you see it, you'll never make it through the night." She was onto something.

In a world that is not yet redeemed, it can get so dark that we can think the sun will never rise and shine again. When it is that dark, we need hope to light our path.

Kingdom hope guides us when it is dark. We can know that the Light of the world rose from the dead and that he will climb over the horizon of life and eventually drive back the night.

KINGDOM HOPE GUIDES
US WHEN IT IS DARK.

Let me tell you a story about my friend Colby. He lived with kingdom hope. We became friends in his freshman year of high school. He loved playing football, he liked school, and he chilled with his friends, especially Benjamin. He was living a typical teenage life until the bad headaches started. His headaches would not go away, and got increasingly worse. His parents took him to see the doctor. Then another doctor. Eventually, a brain scan revealed a tumor, and the biopsy of the tumor revealed a rare, incurable cancer.

Colby's parents called me, their pastor. I was not ready to hear this news. What do you say to parents when their child is given a death sentence? Over the years, I have learned to say nothing, but stay present. My presence with them was more important than my words to them. They asked me to go to the hospital with them as they broke the news to Colby.

Colby's father is a mountain of a man. With a trembling, yet firm, reassuring voice, he told Colby the devastating news. In that moment, I had the honor of witnessing a mother and father walk with Jesus and cling to the hope that is realized as citizens of Abba's kingdom. In the darkness, I saw light in that moment.

I watched Colby and his family walk through the valley of the shadow of death. Every Sunday, there was Colby and his family worshiping and receiving the Word. Colby dove into Scripture with his football teammate, Benjamin. They often prayed together and trusted Jesus together. Every step of the journey Benjamin was there with Colby.

Colby and Benjamin were a living portrait of discipleship, spiritual friendship, and kingdom hope.

As Colby's condition worsened and the pain increased to an unbearable state, he struggled. He wondered if all this Jesus stuff was real. His faith was shaken. He shared his fears with his parents, and his mother called her sister's friends to pray for Colby. The next morning, he woke and said Jesus had visited him. Hope himself reassured Colby. I don't know exactly what Colby meant by that or what precisely happened, but I know after that encounter with Jesus, Colby had an unexplainable peace.

As Colby's mobility decreased, his faith and hope in Jesus increased. Eventually, the time came for Colby to see Jesus face-to-face. But before he left his family to be with Jesus, he asked his father to call me over to his house. He wanted to celebrate the Lord's Supper one last time on this side of eternity. I gathered with the family. Jesus was in our midst. The Spirit was present. Abba was smiling. We received the bread and wine.

We worshiped.

We praised.

We cried.

We laughed.

We delighted in the hope of God's present and future kingdom.

Cancer could not steal Colby's praise. And it surely did not take his life!

Death does not have the last word. Jesus does.

And he says, "I am the resurrection and the life. The one who believes in me, even if he dies, will live. Everyone who lives and believes in me will never die. Do you believe this?" (John 11:25–26). Abba does not promise us that our hearts will not be crushed, but he does promise to bottle our every tear and walk with us through every fear. Kingdom hope is knowing that "in fact, we are confident, and we would prefer to be away from the body and at home with the Lord" (2 Cor. 5:8) and "Death has been swallowed up in [the] victory" of Jesus (1 Cor. 15:54). The next time we see Colby he will be in a resurrected, glorified body in a resurrected, new creation.

ABBA DOES NOT PROMISE US THAT OUR HEARTS WILL NOT BE CRUSHED, BUT HE DOES PROMISE TO BOTTLE OUR EVERY TEAR AND WALK WITH US THROUGH EVERY FEAR.

> Then I heard a loud voice from the throne: Look, God's dwelling is with humanity, and he will live with them. They will be his peoples, and God himself will be with them and will be their God. He will wipe away every tear from their eyes. Death will be no more; grief, crying, and pain will be no more because the previous things have passed away. (Rev. 21:3–4)

When we pray "your kingdom come . . . on earth as it is in heaven," we are praying to enter the story of God's kingdom. It is a story that has a happy, eternal ending in the new heavens and new earth.

God, do you hear me?

———————— Marinate on This ————————

Prayer

Abba,

Engulf me with a desire to see your kingdom
come to earth as it is in heaven.

Align my will to yours.

Your kingdom is no longer a mystery.

Jesus is the kingdom of God.

The way he lived and loved.

The way he healed and cried.

The way he washed his disciples' dirty feet.

The way he broke down racial and gender barriers
to transform a Samaritan woman's life.

The way he was a friend to sinners like me.

The way he cleansed the temple of corrupt money changers.

The way he took the forgotten and made them known.

The way he left the ninety-nine to find the one.

The way he died.

The way he rose from the dead.

The way he will come again.

Jesus is the kingdom of God on full display.

Abba,

May his life, his ways, his attitude be mine.

And may the hope of your future kingdom give
power in the present to live out your kingdom.

In Jesus' name, amen.

Questions for Reflection

1. What new observation did you take from the biblical story line
   from the way it was retold at the beginning of this chapter?

2. Define the kingdom of God in your own words.

3. How does the Lord's Prayer relate to the kingdom? What does it
   mean to pray, "your kingdom come on earth as it is in heaven"?

4. How does the knowledge of the kingdom empower us to live
   today?

Things to Remember

1. Like DNA, the sin sickness of the original man and woman is
   passed into the genes of all their descendants.

2. The king sent his own son to restore and establish his kingdom
   on earth.

3. When you pray the Lord's Prayer, you are praying to know the king, to enter and *participate* in the kingdom, and to be *transformed* into the image of the king.

4. Abba does not promise us that our hearts will not be crushed, but he does promise to bottle our every tear and walk with us through every fear.

CHAPTER 8

Proclaiming Abba's Kingdom

I have never really understood the fascination with the British royal family. What do they do exactly? I know they're a big deal, not just in England, but all over the world. Queen Elizabeth II is among the top ten brand images globally.[1] Her children and grandchildren are megastars as well. The late Princess Diana continues to be famous more than twenty years after her tragic death. But frankly, I just don't get it.

Recently, the royal wedding of Prince Harry and Meghan Markle was like something out of a Disney movie. I am not usually into that type of pageantry, but this former NFL player was moved by its beauty. The entire wedding was like poetry in motion. I shed a few tears. (Okay, more than a few tears).

Why all this fascination? Why the emotion from a guy who isn't fascinated by it? I suspect our fascination with the royal family creates an echo that reverberates in our souls, reminding us of our own royalty.

Hold that thought.

Don't move too fast.

Sit in it for a moment.

---

[1] Christopher Lee, "Prince George Will Never Be King," October 25, 2013, cited in https://newrepublic.com/article/115358/why-prince-george -will-never-be-king (accessed October 21, 2020).

Marinate.

If Abba is the king of the kingdom and you are his child through faith in Christ Jesus, what does that make you? It makes you royalty. The nanosecond you trusted Jesus as your Savior, your status as a rebel against the kingdom was upgraded to royalty. Your royalty is not determined by your worth. It is determined by your new birth.

> **IF ABBA IS THE KING OF THE KINGDOM AND YOU ARE HIS CHILD THROUGH FAITH IN CHRIST JESUS, WHAT DOES THAT MAKE YOU? IT MAKES YOU ROYALTY.**

> But to all who believed him and accepted him, he gave the right to become children of God. They are reborn—not with a physical birth resulting from human passion or plan, but a birth that comes from God. (John 1:12–13 NLT)

When you are born into the British royal family, you are born into the privilege and responsibility of proclaiming the kingdom of Great Britain. They have the privilege of being born royal, being supported financially by tax money and a gigantic family fortune, but there is also great responsibility. The royal family's "prime duty is to produce at least one heir to the throne. Each heir has to provide a child that will guarantee the survival of a monarchy that began with Athelstan, the first king of all-England in 926."[2] The family also has an important role to play in supporting charities, hosting

---

[2] Lee, "Prince George Will Never Be King."

heads of state, presenting citizen awards, appearing at events, and traveling the globe to strengthen diplomatic relationships. The queen opens each session of parliament in person as well.[3]

When we are born into Abba's kingdom as royal priests, our new redemptive status gives us a sacred privilege and responsibility of proclaiming God's kingdom. Because of our new birth, we have a new worth that is equal to Jesus himself. His life, ministry, and mission are now ours. Our life is hidden in his life.

> **WHEN WE ARE BORN INTO ABBA'S KINGDOM AS ROYAL PRIESTS, OUR NEW REDEMPTIVE STATUS GIVES US A SACRED PRIVILEGE AND RESPONSIBILITY OF PROCLAIMING GOD'S KINGDOM.**

> For you died, and your life is hidden with Christ in God. (Col. 3:3)

When we pray "your kingdom come . . . on earth as it is in heaven," we are praying to understand and live out our privilege and responsibility in his kingdom as his royal priests.

Baptized into Royalty

In the Greco-Roman first-century world of Jesus, a fabric maker would change the color of clothing by dipping it into a dye. When the clothing emerged, it was transformed. Similarly, the

---

[3] Caroline Praderio, "Here's What the Royal Family Actually Does Every Day," June 14, 2017, cited in https://www.insider.com/what-does -the-royal-family-do-2017-1 (accessed October 21, 2020).

physical act of baptism symbolizes the internal, eternal reality of dying with Christ and rising to new life with him. By faith in Jesus, God the Holy Spirit dips you into his sinless life, blood, and resurrection and you emerge anew.

> This means that anyone who belongs to Christ has become a new person. The old life is gone; a new life has begun! (2 Cor. 5:17 NLT)

You are royalty because you are clothed in the Royal One, King Jesus himself.

> For those of you who were baptized into Christ have been clothed with Christ. (Gal. 3:27)

Your new birth gives you a life worth living. You are born again into kingdom privilege and responsibility as a royal priest.

As Abba's kid, you have the privilege and responsibility of partnering with him to bring heaven to earth and proclaim its arrival. Adam and Eve were the original royal family with a sacred purpose. N. T. Wright said,

> The main task of this vocation is in "image-bearing," reflecting the Creator's wise stewardship into the world and reflecting the praises of all creation back to its maker. Those who do so are the "Royal Priesthood," the "Kingdom of Priests," the people who are called to stand at the dangerous but exhilarating point where heaven and earth meet.[4]

---

[4] N. T. Wright, *The Day the Revolution Began* (San Francisco: HarperOne, 2016), 76.

Abba's goal is not simply to send us to "heaven" when we die. Abba's holy purpose is to renew our sacred purpose of being royal priests in his creation. We are the people infused with Abba's life to do his work on earth (1 Cor. 3:9).

Adam and Eve were the first royal priests or image-bearers. We saw how they abandoned their calling and rebelled against God instead. But God was still working, and called Abraham, a decisive step in his plans to redeem the world. Later God freed his people, Abraham's offspring, from slavery in Egypt so that they could fulfill their sacred purpose.

> Moses went up the mountain to God, and the LORD called to him from the mountain: "This is what you must say to the house of Jacob and explain to the Israelites: 'You have seen what I did to the Egyptians and how I carried you on eagles' wings and brought you to myself. Now if you will carefully listen to me and keep my covenant, you will be my own possession out of all the peoples, although the whole earth is mine, and you will be *my kingdom of priests* and my holy nation.' These are the words that you are to say to the Israelites." (Exod. 19:3–6, emphasis mine)

Please note that entrance into God's kingdom and status as royal priests are gifts of Abba's grace. He says, "You have seen what I did to the Egyptians and how I carried you on eagles' wings and brought you to myself" (Exod. 19:4). The Hebrew people didn't escape Egypt by their own power, nor did they do enough good works to earn God's favor, to force God's hand in saving them. His salvation of them was purely of grace.

Grace is what Abba does for us.

Grace is not just a New Testament reality.

From Genesis to Revelation, grace shouts from the rooftops the story of Abba and his love for his kids.

ENTRANCE INTO GOD'S KINGDOM AND STATUS AS ROYAL PRIESTS ARE GIFTS OF ABBA'S GRACE.

Grace is the oxygen that keeps Abba's kids alive.

Then in King Jesus, "we have all received grace upon grace from his fullness" (John 1:16). King Jesus sets humanity free *from* slavery to sin and death for a sacred purpose: royal priesthood.

> But you are a chosen race, a *royal priesthood*, a holy nation, a people for his possession, so that you may proclaim the praises of the one who called you out of darkness into his marvelous light. (1 Pet. 2:9, emphasis mine)

By God's grace, you are included in a new humanity that Peter calls a "chosen race." You are a royal priesthood, a nation of people set apart as Abba's beloved possession. All this grace upon grace is so you may proclaim the praises of the one who called you out of darkness into his marvelous light.

A royal priest is a person enthralled by God's grace and enraptured in praise. Praise is what a person does when they tell the story of God's rescuing grace in their lives.

Prayer is the great adventure of becoming who you were meant to be, exploring the limitless depths of Abba's grace, and proclaiming his love to the world.

Gospel-Vision Takes Shape

The gospel-shaped vision of our sacred purpose comes into focus in the book of Revelation:

> And from Jesus Christ, the faithful witness, the firstborn from the dead and the ruler of the kings of the earth. To him who loves us and has set us free from our sins by his blood, and *made us a kingdom*, priests to his God and Father—to him be glory and dominion forever and ever. Amen. (Rev. 1:5–6, emphasis mine)

And they sang a new song:
> You are worthy to take the scroll
> and to open its seals,
> because you were slaughtered,
> and you purchased people
> for God by your blood
> from every tribe and language
> and people and nation.
> You made them a *kingdom*
> *and priests* to our God,
> and they will reign on the earth.
> (Rev. 5:9–10, emphasis mine)

Blessed and holy is the one who shares in the first
resurrection! The second death has no power over
them, but they will be *priests of God and of Christ*,
and they will reign with him for a thousand years.
(Rev. 20:6, emphasis mine)

You see, you are royalty. The British royal family has nothing
on you.

You are Abba's kid.

By grace, Abba, in Christ, has *made* you a royal priest in his
kingdom. In the Spirit's power, you have the sacred task of embodying the kingdom on earth. What the evil one stole from you, Jesus
reclaimed and restored. He gave you your birthright back.

This changes everything about the way we live. We have a new
vision, a new mission, a new purpose in life. One of the best ways we
can live into that purpose is to see how others have done so. I want
to introduce you to some of Abba's kids who live out their privilege
and responsibility as his royal priests.

Abba Does Not Need Your Ability, Just Your Availability

Kristel's Story

Kristel grew up in an immigrant Catholic family from Central
America. Her parents risked their lives and their children's lives
to come to America. Their country was being torn apart by war.
They wanted better for their children, so they came to the country
founded by immigrants for immigrants, America.

Expectations were set early on for Kristel. She would be obedient, get good grades, make sure not to waste her future, and attend Mass on Sundays.

In high school, after six months of being invited by a friend to come with her to youth group, she finally went. She encountered Jesus in a beautiful, life-transforming way. Over the years, her passion for Jesus, theology, and writing grew. She wanted to pour her life out for the sake of Jesus and his kingdom. Kristel wanted others to experience grace the way she had.

Kristel has a beautiful mind with a passion for theology and writing. She wanted to develop her theological understanding, so she asked her pastor about going to seminary. Unfortunately, sitting in her pastor's office, she was discouraged from attending seminary. Seminary was for men, according to him. She went anyway. However, while at seminary, a professor told a class that she was in that women should never learn more theology than their husbands because their spouses would feel threatened. Despite these discouragements, she pressed on.

Kristel has an introverted personality. She is a thinker who likes to wrestle with deep thoughts about the serious matters of life. Because of her personality, some ministry leaders in her church context questioned if a person like her could be in ministry. These negative experiences left her discouraged, but she did not give up. Kristel resisted and trusted that Abba had a purpose for her in his kingdom that could utilize her mind, personality, and gifting.

By God's grace, Kristel is now on staff at Transformation Church, serving in her gifting. She uses her writing gift to create curriculum in both Spanish and English to equip God's other royal priests and those who have yet to come to Jesus. She teaches theology in Spanish for our Spanish-speaking members. She is also on my book writing team, adding insights to make my books—including this one!—better.

In God's kingdom, whether you are male or female, immigrant or native born, rich, middle class, or poor, introvert or extrovert, you are a royal priest. Abba gives us *participating grace* to participate in Christ and to participate in his kingdom as his royal priests. The apostle Paul writes, "But anyone joined to the Lord is one spirit with him" (1 Cor. 6:17). The word *joined* gives the imagery of entering a sacred covenant with Abba through his Son, by his Spirit. Just like a marriage union, the person in union with Abba forsakes all other unions because his or her life now belongs to God. Because you and Kristel are joined to Jesus, his resources and his sacred purpose are yours. You are a royal priest in the King's kingdom. Grace gives you space in this place called the kingdom of Abba.

Wini's Story

Wini grew up in a conservative, Southern churchgoing family. She followed the rules as best she could. She was indoctrinated in a version of Christianity that did not talk much about Jesus' redemptive work of grace. The teaching she received was more about how to not let Jesus down and make sure to uphold cultural Christianity's rules.

During Wini's freshman year of college, she got pregnant. She returned home, but at her church, she felt looked down upon and shamed. Wini became the example of what good Christian girls did not do. She felt abandoned, rejected, and neglected. However, one friend stood by her, helping her through what was a very challenging time as she put her child up for adoption.

Over the years, Abba's grace erased her shame, silenced her guilt, and cast out her feelings of condemnation. In 2010, Wini, her husband, and their young family helped start Transformation Church. I immediately noticed her servant's heart. She especially had a tender spot for the forgotten, neglected, and rejected. Because Jesus met Wini in her pain and shame and brought her through, her heart became a garden of grace for the brokenhearted.

> The LORD is near the brokenhearted;
> he saves those crushed in spirit. (Ps. 34:18)

I knew that if Transformation Church was going to transform our community, serving our local public schools was essential. I brought Wini with me to meet with public school officials in the area. As we began to talk to the school administrators, I asked Wini to share the heart of why we wanted to serve teachers, students, and administrators. Within about twenty seconds of Wini opening her mouth, I saw the gift. I saw her heart of compassion. I saw the love of Christ compelling her. As I witnessed this moment, I shut up and asked her to continue sharing the vision of Transformation Church and our desire to serve our public schools.

Since that moment ten years ago, Transformation Church has prepared nearly 400,000 backpack meals to feed children over the weekend who otherwise would not have enough food to eat. Through Wini's leadership, we have bought computers for schools and helped develop a leadership program within several of the public schools with which we partner. Since the pandemic of 2020, we have made nearly 500,000 meals for families in need who have been impacted by the recession. She also leads our pro-life ministry initiatives to help mothers and fathers navigate the difficulties of pregnancy—a truly beautiful thing considering the support she did not have when she was in the same position.

Wini is a royal priest, expressing the kingdom of Abba through serving our public schools and other ministries that meet the physical and spiritual needs of people. In Wini, I see the redeeming grace of King Jesus. Abba's grace in Jesus is so extensive that everyone is redeemable. He will take anyone and remake them into a royal priest. The kingdom is open to all.

> **ABBA'S GRACE IN JESUS IS SO EXTENSIVE THAT EVERYONE IS REDEEMABLE. HE WILL TAKE ANYONE AND REMAKE THEM INTO A ROYAL PRIEST. THE KINGDOM IS OPEN TO ALL.**

> In him we have redemption through his blood, the forgiveness of our trespasses, according to the riches of his grace that he richly poured out on us with all wisdom and understanding. (Eph. 1:7–8)

Paul's Story

I met Paul in 2009 when we were in the dreaming and planning stages of forming Transformation Church. As our planting team explored the New Testament, we were under the conviction that the Lord wanted us to plant a multiethnic church that was captivated by Jesus, his kingdom, and his gospel. In the New Testament, and in the life of Jesus himself, we saw Abba's heart for justice, mercy, reaching the lost, racial justice and racial reconciliation, and discipleship. Everything was going according to plan except for the fact that I needed an executive pastor with experience to help bring our dreams into reality. I needed an older, wiser ministry leader who loved Jesus and people and who had the unique ability to mentor me in the art of leading a church.

While preaching in Colorado, I shared with some ministry friends my idea about starting a church. They asked me if I knew Paul Allen. Paul was an experienced executive pastor who also happened to live in the Charlotte, North Carolina, area. When I got back to town, I connected with him and shared my heart. After we met, I sent him my pitiful church planting prospective and asked him to review it and let me know what he thought. A few days went by and he sent me back an email that said the perspective looked great. The only thing we were missing was an "old, bald white guy." I immediately called him. We met at a coffee shop and poured out our hearts.

Before he agreed to be the executive pastor, I told him that I was scheduled to make $68,000 the upcoming year *if* the church plant worked out. I then told him I would be willing to split my salary with him, but there was only one problem—it was imaginary money. It didn't exist yet. He looked at me and said, "I'm in." I said, "Did you hear what I said? The money does not exist." He said, "Yes, I heard you." Pastor Paul was my first hire. I hired him with imaginary money, but the vision of Transformation Church was real. As he entered the fourth quarter of ministry life, he was ready for a new challenge and an opportunity to serve and be a part of the church that I had described to him. He also asked me if I would pastor him. For most of his ministry, he was used for his gift, but not appreciated and discipled for the gift that he is as a person. I said it would be my honor to pastor him. In the early days of Transformation Church, I leaned into his experience to serve and lead.

When I think of Pastor Paul, he reminds me that Abba gives his children *incorporating grace* so their unique gifts can be expressed in and through the church, and so Abba's kingdom can come to earth as it is in heaven. Paul is winsome, brilliant, kind, and compassionate. He understands how to shepherd God's people. He is a royal priest.

> Now as we have many parts in one body, and all the parts do not have the same function, in the same way, we who are many are one body in Christ and individually members of one another. (Rom. 12:4–5)

When we pray "your kingdom come . . . on earth as it is in heaven," we are praying to enter and grasp our sacred purpose of being a royal priest in the kingdom. We are royalty. The mystery of prayer is our hearts joining to Abba's heart and becoming who we were meant to be: royal priests.

THE MYSTERY OF PRAYER IS OUR HEARTS JOINING TO ABBA'S HEART AND BECOMING WHO WE WERE MEANT TO BE: ROYAL PRIESTS.

──────────── Marinate on This ────────────

Prayer

Abba,

How can it be that I am royalty?

How can it be that someone with my past can be a royal priest?

How can it be that you would use me to declare your glory?

The only way this can be true is that the way, the truth, and life,
sacrificed his life to clothe me in his royal robes of righteousness.

Help me, Holy Spirit, to sing with the psalmist,
"I rejoice greatly in the Lord,
I exult in my God;
for he has clothed me with the garments of salvation
and wrapped me in a robe of righteousness" (Isa. 61:10).

Abba,

Help me to see that I am who you say that I am, "a chosen race,
a royal priesthood, a holy nation, a people for his possession,
so that you may proclaim the praises of the one who called
you out of darkness into his marvelous light" (1 Pet. 2:9).

Abba,

Help me to see that it is your grace that created
space and gave me a place in your kingdom.

God, do you hear me?

Thank you for the privilege and responsibility of proclaiming your kingdom on earth as it is in heaven as your royal priest.

In Jesus' name, amen.

Questions for Reflection

1. Why does it seem like human beings are hardwired for fascination with royalty?

2. What does it mean to be a "royal priest"? How does that inform our mission in the world?

3. Which story that Derwin shared about friends who live into their purpose as royal priests stood out most to you? Who is a person in your life who is living out their purpose as a royal priest? What can you do to be around people like this and learn from them?

Things to Remember

1. If Abba is the king of the kingdom and you are his child through faith in Christ Jesus, what does that make you? It makes you royalty.

2. Entrance into God's kingdom and status as royal priests are gifts of Abba's grace.

3. We have a new vision, a new mission, a new purpose in life. One of the best ways we can live into that purpose is to see how others have done so.

4. The mystery of prayer is our hearts joining to Abba's heart and becoming who we were meant to be: royal priests.

CHAPTER 9

Abba's Kids Personify the Kingdom

 When we join God on mission for his kingdom as his royal priests, we also gain other roles in the kingdom. We begin to personify the kingdom as members of his chosen family, as Christ's bride, as the Spirit's holy temple, and ultimately as his hands and feet—the church.

We Are God's Family

We all crave to belong to a family where we are loved and known. We all desire a people of our own who will have our backs. This holy longing is strong because we are made in the image and the likeness of God. Abba, the Son, and the Holy Spirit are an eternal community of self-giving love. When this eternal community created humanity, God invited us to join his family.

Long ago, this God promised Abraham a single, worldwide, multiethnic family of unity and community.

ABBA, THE SON, AND THE HOLY SPIRIT ARE AN ETERNAL COMMUNITY OF SELF-GIVING LOVE. WHEN THIS ETERNAL COMMUNITY CREATED HUMANITY, GOD INVITED US TO JOIN HIS FAMILY.

In Abba's family, there are to be no unknown ones or forgotten ones, just loved ones.

In Abba's family, there is to be no racism, oppression, or unwanted babies.

In Abba's family, women and men are to be coequal and coheirs in the kingdom.

> What's more, the Scriptures looked forward to this time when God would make the Gentiles right in his sight because of their faith. God proclaimed this good news to Abraham long ago when he said, "All nations will be blessed through you." So all who put their faith in Christ share the same blessing Abraham received because of his faith. (Gal. 3:8–9 NLT)

God's redeeming work began with a certain people—the physical offspring of Abraham. But these people, the Israelites, were never to be a *cul de sac* of God's blessing; they were to be a conduit of God's blessing to the whole world. They were blessed to be a blessing.

Now, in Christ, "there is no longer Jew or Gentile, slave or free, male and female. For you are all one in Christ Jesus. And now that you belong to Christ, you are the true children of Abraham. You are his heirs, and God's promise to Abraham belongs to you" (Gal. 3:28–29 NLT).

When we pray "your kingdom come . . . on earth as it is in heaven," we are praying a prayer of gratitude. We are grateful that Abba is faithful to keep his promise to Abraham through the person and work of Jesus. We are Abba's kids, who are, in Christ, the dwelling place of God the Holy Spirit.

> The purpose was that the blessing of Abraham would come to the Gentiles by Christ Jesus, so that we could receive the promised Spirit through faith. (Gal. 3:14)

We are praying a prayer of gratitude because we have a new family of origin that originates in the heart of Abba.

> Even before he made the world, God loved us and chose us in Christ to be holy and without fault in his eyes. God decided in advance to adopt us into his own family by bringing us to himself through Jesus Christ. This is what he wanted to do, and it gave him great pleasure. (Eph. 1:4–5 NLT)

We Are Christ's Bride

There is a rumor going around that my wife and I are dancing machines. It's true!

Since Vicki and I no longer go to the club, we display our dancing skills at weddings. We love weddings. The joy, the celebration, and the music! At the last wedding I officiated, the bride and groom hired a DJ and a mariachi band. We went from doing the Electric Slide and the Running Man to traditional South Texas Mexican dancing. Vicki and I *scorched* the dance floor.

But as much as I might think we steal the show with our dancing, the highlight of every wedding is when the bride walks down the aisle. The guests stand on tiptoe to admire her beauty and dazzling dress. The preacher and the groom await the bride at the altar. When a man and woman in Christ "jump the broom" and get married, they enter a sacred covenant that reveals how Jesus loves his church.

> Husbands, love your wives, just as Christ loved the church and gave himself for her to make her holy, cleansing her with the washing of water by the word. He did this to present the church to himself in splendor, without spot or wrinkle or anything like that, but holy and blameless. (Eph. 5:25–27)

The physical act of marriage is a living portrait of how we are the bride of Christ. Just as Abba has always longed to have a family, the Son has always longed to have a bride. In Abba's kingdom, we are not only his family, but we are also the Son's bride.

Jesus loves you.

Jesus protects you.

Jesus cares for you.

Jesus provides for you.

Jesus is for you.

You are the bride of Christ, along with all your brothers and sisters in the church.

When we pray "your kingdom come . . . on earth as it is in heaven," it is a reminder that we have entered a sacred covenant with Jesus. We are his betrothed. He is preparing us for his return, which will culminate in the grand wedding feast with his church.

Instead of buying a wedding ring, he bought us with a blood-stained cross and an empty tomb.

What do we give Jesus in return for such lavish love? We give Jesus our loyalty. We give Jesus our lives and show this covenant commitment by being baptized and living a life of obedience.

> Therefore, brothers and sisters, in view of the mer-
> cies of God, I urge you to present your bodies as
> a living sacrifice, holy and pleasing to God; this is
> your true worship. (Rom. 12:1)

We Are the Spirit's Temple

Written into our souls is a desire for something sacred. Even devout atheists and agnostics are searching for the sacred. Many of them speak and write about astrophysics, biology, and natural selection with the fervor of Southern tent-revivalist preachers. They speak with reverence of these topics, because all of us are looking for something to worship.

**EVEN DEVOUT ATHEISTS AND
AGNOSTICS ARE SEARCHING
FOR THE SACRED.**

Before Jesus found and rescued me, football was sacred to me. It was my functional god. It gave me community, a band of brothers to call family and a common purpose bigger than myself. No matter who we are, or when we are, or where we are, our craving for the sacred will be present.

> From one man he has made every nationality to
> live over the whole earth and has determined their
> appointed times and the boundaries of where they
> live. He did this so that they might seek God,
> and perhaps they might reach out and find him,

though he is not far from each one of us. (Acts
17:26–27)

There is a common cultural myth that some people are just "not
religious." They're above the fray of religion, not in need of the "opi-
ate of the masses." But don't be fooled: everyone is religious. If we do
not give our allegiance to the uncreated Creator revealed in the merciful person of Messiah Jesus, we will give it to something, and we
will "be enticed and led astray by mute idols" (1 Cor. 12:2). Behind
every idol—every religious or so-called "secular" commitment apart
from Christ—are dark powers of evil that seek to destroy us.

We long for the sacred because we were created to dwell with
the Sacred One. And the good news for Christians is that, we do. In
fact, the Sacred One dwells with—and *within*—us. We are not only
Abba's family, the Son's bride, but we are also the dwelling place of
God the Spirit.

> So, then, you are no longer foreigners and strang-
> ers, but fellow citizens with the saints, and mem-
> bers of God's household, built on the foundation
> of the apostles and prophets, with Christ Jesus
> himself as the cornerstone. In him the whole
> building, being put together, grows into a holy
> temple in the Lord. In him you are also being
> built together for God's dwelling the Spirit. (Eph.
> 2:19–22)

Our cravings for a family, marriage,[1] and sacredness are ultimately satisfied by Abba through his Son, as the Spirit indwells and seals us in the promised family of Abraham. When we pray "your kingdom come . . . on earth as it is in heaven," we are reminding ourselves that as Abba's kids, we are participating in a family of royal priests, who are the bride of Christ Jesus, and the sacred dwelling place of God.

This is our new identity.

Our identity determines our function in the world.

When we know who we are and whose we are in Christ Jesus, our roots grow down deep into the soil of Yahweh's gracious, unchanging, eternal love.

AS ABBA'S KIDS, WE ARE PARTICIPATING IN A FAMILY OF ROYAL PRIESTS, WHO ARE THE BRIDE OF CHRIST JESUS, AND THE SACRED DWELLING PLACE OF GOD.

> For this reason I kneel before the Father from whom every family in heaven and on earth is named. I pray that he may grant you, according to the riches of his glory, to be strengthened with power in your inner being through his Spirit, and that Christ may dwell in your hearts through faith. I pray that you, being rooted and firmly

---

[1] If you are single and have a desire to serve Jesus through singleness, this does not make you a second-class Christian. You are married to Christ and your redemptive purposes are the same as those within the family of God who are married.

established in love, may be able to comprehend with all the saints what is the length and width, height and depth of God's love, and to know Christ's love that surpasses knowledge, so that you may be filled with all the fullness of God. Now to him who is able to do above and beyond all that we ask or think according to the power that works in us—to him be glory in the church and in Christ Jesus to all generations, forever and ever. Amen. (Eph. 3:14–21)

We Are the Body of Christ

Abba declares that you are a precious child in his family, the beautiful, holy bride of his Son, and the sacred dwelling place of God the Holy Spirit. Another life-giving name you receive when you enter the kingdom of God by allegiance to King Jesus is the body of Christ, the Church. Abba's kids are the Church.

Now you are the body of Christ, and individual members of it. (1 Cor. 12:27)

One of the coolest things that ever happened to me took place years ago at a Brigham Young University football game. I was back at my alma mater, reminiscing on the field right before the game, and a former teammate joined me and asked me what I was doing now. I told him that I was a pastor-theologian. His mouth dropped open. He said, "You are a what?" I said, "Yeah, man, I am a pastor-theologian. Can you believe that?" I will never forget his next words, "Dewey, I am going to start reading my Bible more. You are a pastor-theologian. Wow!"

My former teammate was shocked because he remembers me before I met Jesus. In college, he and I were assigned to speak to a Mormon youth group as a means of community service for the team. He was a returning Mormon missionary, so he was used to public speaking. He remembers how badly I stuttered attempting to speak to those kids. He also remembered that in college I had no interest in spiritual things.

But Jesus met me in the middle of that, and Jesus will meet you in your mess. He can transform anyone, including a hard-line, nationalistic, pharisaical Jewish religious scholar named Paul.

Paul described himself as "circumcised the eighth day; of the nation of Israel, of the tribe of Benjamin, a Hebrew born of Hebrews; regarding the law, a Pharisee; regarding zeal, persecuting the church; regarding the righteousness that is in the law, blameless" (Phil. 3:5–6). If anyone was a proud, ethnocentric Jew, it was Paul.

In fact, Paul was so zealous for Israel and his version of pharisaic Judaism that he ravaged the church (Acts 8:3). The word *ravaged* means to "disgrace as by insult, treat with indignity, injure, or destroy." Paul wanted to destroy the family of God, the bride of Christ, the temple of the Holy Spirit. But Abba, who is gracious to the undeserving, transformed him into the greatest missionary in the history of the church he once tried to destroy.

> They simply kept hearing, "He who formerly persecuted us now preaches the faith he once tried to destroy." And they glorified God because of me. (Gal. 1:23–24)

For the apostles Paul, Peter, and John, and for Jesus himself, the Church is how Christ expresses his kingdom on earth.

He has rescued us from the domain of darkness and transferred us into the kingdom of the Son he loves. In him we have redemption, the forgiveness of sins. (Col. 1:13–14)

To him who loves us and has set us free from our sins by his blood, and made us a kingdom, priests to his God and Father—to him be glory and dominion forever and ever. Amen. (Rev. 1:5–6)

Simon Peter answered, "You are the Messiah, the Son of the living God." Jesus responded, "Blessed are you, Simon son of Jonah, because flesh and blood did not reveal this to you, but my Father in heaven. And I also say to you that you are Peter, and on this rock I will build my church, and the gates of Hades will not overpower it. I will give you the keys of the kingdom of heaven, and whatever you bind on earth will have been bound in heaven, and whatever you loose on earth will have been loosed in heaven." (Matt. 16:16–19)

My doctoral advisor, New Testament scholar Scot McKnight, writes, "There is no kingdom now outside the Church."[2]

Jesus is the kingdom of God embodied in human form. The Church is the body of Christ personified on earth. Therefore, the kingdom of God is expressed only through the Church, that is, the people who have allegiance to King Jesus.

---

[2] Scot McKnight, *Kingdom Conspiracy* (Grand Rapids: Brazos Press, 2014), 87.

THE KINGDOM OF GOD IS EXPRESSED ONLY THROUGH THE CHURCH, THAT IS, THE PEOPLE WHO HAVE ALLEGIANCE TO KING JESUS.

When we pray "your kingdom come . . . on earth as it is in heaven," we are deepening our awareness to the privilege of being the physical body through which King Jesus reveals his kingdom. We also move from self-centric prayers to kingdom-centric prayers. We are agreeing that Jesus does not exist to bring our kingdoms to earth but that we exist to bring his kingdom to earth.

> For everything was created by him,
> in heaven and on earth,
> the visible and the invisible,
> whether thrones or dominions
> or rulers or authorities—
> all things have been created
> through him and for him.
> He is before all things,
> and by him all things hold together.
> He is also the head of the body, the church.
> (Col. 1:16–18)

In fulfilling our sacred purpose of embodying the kingdom of God, we experience the fulfillment for which we were created.

> "Blessed are those who hunger and thirst for righteousness, for they will be filled."[3] (Matt. 5:6)

---

[3] See my book, *The Good Life: What Jesus Teaches about Finding True Happiness* (Nashville: B&H Publishing, 2020).

When we pray "your kingdom come . . . on earth as it is in heaven," we are attuning our hearts to the reality that Abba expresses his kingdom through his family, his Son's bride, the dwelling place of the Spirit (the church). That is you. That is me. That is one single, multicolored, multi-class, multigenerational people promised to Abraham. We are binding our wills to his will. Every day and every thing becomes pregnant with divine possibilities for the King of glory to be glorious to you, in you, and through you.

Do everything for the glory of God. (1 Cor. 10:31b)

The Church—that is the single, transcultural family that Abba promised Abraham, that Jesus bought with his blood, and that the Spirit sealed—is how Abba displays his glory on earth (Eph. 1:13–14).

Slow down.

Reread that sentence.

Understanding this kingdom reality will shape your reality to align with Abba's.

This Jesus-centered perspective will give you a new outlook on prayer and life that aligns with Jesus.

What Is the Church?

The Church—that is you, that is me, that is all of our brothers and sisters in Messiah Jesus—is important to Abba.

The Church is Abba's family.

The Church is the Son's bride.

The Church is the Spirit's dwelling place.

The Church is the blood-bought, new people of God, who are a Spirit-sealed community of royal priests. The Church stands at the dangerous, adventurous crossroads of heaven and earth. It has the privilege and sacred responsibility of doing the King's bidding on earth. The Church is God's living presence on earth.

Wherever the apostle Paul preached the gospel, new communities of Jews and Gentiles came into being because of their incorporation into Christ Jesus. Even though the word *ekklésia* (church) appears only three times in the Gospels, it originated in the earliest Jerusalem church as a self-designation of Jesus' followers. The term *ekklésia* resonated with Gentiles who would have understood the church as a new kind of civic gathering.

In the ancient world of Paul, just like in our cultures, the Greco-Roman world was separated along lines of ethnicity (race), class, and gender. The gospel that Paul preached not only forgave sins but created a family with different colored skins, where oneness and unity were created in Christ. The cross of Christ Jesus broke down the ancient, sinful social barriers that divided people to form a countercultural community of racial reconciliation and racial justice that was unrivaled in the ancient world.

I believe we can do it again as we learn to pray and obey.

> For Christ himself has brought peace to us. He united Jews and Gentiles into one people when, in his own body on the cross, he broke down the wall of hostility that separated us. (Eph. 2:14 NLT)

> Give no offense to Jews or Greeks or the church of God, just as I also try to please everyone in everything, not seeking my own benefit, but the benefit of many, so that they may be saved. (1 Cor. 10:32–33)

For Paul, Peter, John, and Jesus, the church is the fulfilled promise that Abba made to Abraham. Abba's family, the Son's bride, and the Spirit's dwelling, that is, the Church, is to be a foretaste of ultimate redemption to come in the new heavens and new earth. As a kingdom of priests, we are to personify to the world what love, reconciliation, justice, peace, and life look like under the gracious rule of Jesus in Abba's kingdom. Our faithful witness becomes a living invitation to others not yet included in God's kingdom.

AS A KINGDOM OF PRIESTS, WE ARE TO PERSONIFY TO THE WORLD WHAT LOVE, RECONCILIATION, JUSTICE, PEACE, AND LIFE LOOK LIKE UNDER THE GRACIOUS RULE OF JESUS IN ABBA'S KINGDOM.

——————— Marinate on This ———————

Prayer

Abba,

Attune my will to your will.

May your kingdom come to earth as it is in heaven through me.

Help me believe that I am a member of your family, the
bride to your Son, and the dwelling place of the Spirit.

Help me believe that I am who you say I am.

Help me to embrace that I am the church, the
transcultural family you promised Abraham.

I am a part of the people that you show yourself through.

King Jesus,

Release the love and justice of heaven on this hellish
earth through me and my brothers and sisters.

Holy Spirit,

Thank you that I am your sacred place of presence and grace;
faithfully display the kingdom of God in me and through
me for the sake of the world and the glory of Abba.

In the Name of the Father, the Son, and the Spirit,

Amen.

Questions for Reflection

1. What is your experience with "the church"?

2. What new understanding of church did this chapter give you?

3. Which of the metaphors about the Church—the family of God, the bride of Christ, the temple of the Holy Spirit, and the body of Christ—stood out most to you? Why?

4. How does membership in a local church connect us to God's kingdom purposes in the world?

Points to Remember

1. Written into our souls is a desire for something sacred. Even devout atheists and agnostics are searching for the sacred.

2. As Abba's kids, we are participating in a family of royal priests, who are the bride of Christ Jesus, and the sacred dwelling place of God.

3. The kingdom of God is expressed only through the Church, that is, the people who have allegiance to King Jesus.

4. As a kingdom of priests, we are to personify to the world what love, reconciliation, justice, peace, and life look like under the gracious rule of Jesus in Abba's kingdom

CHAPTER 10

Pursuing Abba's Kingdom of Love

No one who has ever walked on the face of the earth has lived a life of love like Jesus.

He perfectly loved his Abba, himself, and other people. When the Scripture says that Jesus was "tempted in every way as we are, yet without sin," it is bearing witness to his life of love (Heb. 4:15). This life was possible because of his unending reliance on the Holy Spirit.

> "If you love me, you will keep my commands. And I will ask the Father, and he will give you another Counselor to be with you forever. He is the Spirit of truth." (John 14:15–17)

Jesus lived a beautiful life. So beautiful that John the Apostle writes this about him,

> So the Word became human and made his home among us. He was full of unfailing love and faithfulness. And we have seen his glory, the glory of the Father's one and only Son. (John 1:14 NLT)

> No one has ever seen God. The one and only Son, who is himself God and is at the Father's side—he has revealed him. (John 1:18)

Jesus lived the life of love you and I were created to live. He revealed the beautiful face and grace of Abba.

> For God who said, "Let light shine out of darkness," has shone in our hearts to give the light of the knowledge of God's glory in the face of Jesus Christ. (2 Cor. 4:6)

The precious gift of salvation is an offer to participate in Abba's divine nature and to pursue his kingdom.

> His divine power has given us everything required for life and godliness through the knowledge of him who called us by his own glory and goodness. By these he has given us very great and precious promises, so that through them you may share in the divine nature, escaping the corruption that is in the world because of evil desire. (2 Pet. 1:3–4)

Our ugliness finds absolution in Jesus' blood. His beautiful life is accredited to us as if we lived it. Because Jesus is the kingdom of God made flesh, the kingdom of God is a kingdom of love.

Love is the cross-shaped tattoo that Abba's kids have engraved in their souls.

Love is so central to the kingdom of God, the apostle John wrote, "The one who does not love does not know God, because God is love" (1 John 4:8).

Often, an anemic version of love is put forth as the real thing. But the real thing is only found in the heart of the real God. He wants to share his love with you. It is the reason you exist—to be loved and to love.

Love is giving.

Love is living.

Love is fulfilling.

Love is sacrificial.

Love is patient beyond reason.

Love is hopeful even when it makes no sense.

Love conquers evil.

Love defeats death.

Love rights the wrongs.

Love bottles every tear.

Love heals the hurt.

Love sets the captives free.

Love lifts the oppressed.

Love humbles the proud.

Love gives grace to the humble.

Love transforms messes into masterpieces.

Love welcomes all the prodigals home.

Love runs after the runaways.

Love is forgiving and sin-killing.

Love looks like a bloody man on a cross.

Love looks like an empty tomb.

Love has a name—Jesus.

> God's love was revealed among us in this way:
> God sent his one and only Son into the world so
> that we might live through him. Love consists in
> this: not that we loved God, but that he loved us
> and sent his Son to be the atoning sacrifice for our
> sins. Dear friends, if God loved us in this way, we
> also must love one another. (1 John 4:9–11)

In response to Abba's love in Christ Jesus, we have the privilege of loving God, ourselves, and people. Just as the cross has a vertical and horizontal beam, we are to love Abba, self, and neighbor. Abba's kids are a cross-shaped, transcultural family of love.

When we pray "your kingdom come . . . on earth as it is in heaven," we are praying "that [we], being rooted and firmly established in love, may be able to comprehend with all the saints what is the length and width, height and depth of God's love, and to know Christ's love that surpasses knowledge, so that [we] may be filled with all the fullness of God" (Eph. 3:17–19).

JUST AS THE CROSS HAS A VERTICAL AND HORIZONTAL BEAM, WE ARE TO LOVE ABBA, SELF, AND NEIGHBOR. ABBA'S KIDS ARE A CROSS-SHAPED, TRANSCULTURAL FAMILY OF LOVE.

We are praying to be filled with the fullness of Abba.

We are praying to pursue who we were meant to be, which means being "imitators of God, as dearly loved children, and walk in love, as Christ also loved us and gave himself for us, a sacrificial and fragrant offering to God" (Eph. 5:1–2).

Let's go back to the ancient world of Jesus, and enroll in his school of love so we can discover how to love our neighbors as ourselves.

Shema

Two thousand years ago, a Jewish expert in the Torah, the first five books of the Bible, tested Jesus. He wanted to prove that this upstart rabbi from the backwater town of Nazareth was a phony:

> Then an expert in the law stood up to test him,
> saying, "Teacher, what must I do to inherit eternal
> life?"
>
> "What is written in the law?" he asked him.
> "How do you read it?"
>
> He answered, "Love the Lord your God with
> all your heart, with all your soul, with all your
> strength, and with all your mind," and "your
> neighbor as yourself."
>
> "You've answered correctly," he told him. "Do
> this and you will live."
>
> But wanting to justify himself, he asked Jesus,
> "And who is my neighbor?" (Luke 10:25–29)

As a faithful Jew, Jesus would have prayed the *Shema* three times every day. The *Shema* is the sacred combination of Deuteronomy 6:4–5 and Leviticus 19:9–18. This prayer is the heart of ancient Judaism and at the core of what it means to follow Jesus as a new covenant family of royal priests, and it informed Jesus' answer to the Pharisee.

A fully formed follower of Jesus is one who is pursuing loving Abba, self, and neighbor through reliance on God the Holy Spirit. When we pray "your kingdom come . . . on earth as it is in heaven," we are praying a prayer that situates us in the atmosphere of loving God, ourselves, and our neighbors. But what does it mean to love our neighbor as ourselves?

The Jewish expert in the Torah discovered quickly that Jesus knew what he was talking about, so he tried to deflect from the truth that was staring him in the face. He said to Jesus, "And who is my neighbor?" (Luke 10:29).

For a first-century Jewish man in the Greco-Roman context, his neighbor would have been another Jew.

That may sound awfully narrow, but before you get self-righteous on the Jewish religious scholar, marinate on this. For four hundred years, Gentiles had held his Jewish ancestors as slaves in Egypt. Then groups of Gentiles named the Canaanites, Hethites, Amorites, Perizzites, Hivites, and Jebusites tried to defeat the Jewish people as they journeyed to the Promised Land. Later, the great Babylonian empire, another group of powerful Gentiles, captured Jews from the Promised Land and exiled them to Babylon. Then the Greek empire harassed the Jews, even desecrating their places of worship. Now, the Roman Empire was oppressing the Jews in Israel.

That is a long history of bad blood.

Now you can see why the religious scholar would have had an ethnocentric attitude. It wasn't like the big kid at school picking on all the little kids; it was like the little kid who always gets picked on and, as a result, doesn't really care for the big kid!

Considering Jewish history with Gentiles, he probably did not think he could trust Gentiles. But it is in this cultural context that Jesus says, "Love your enemies and pray for those who persecute you, so that you may be children of your Father in heaven" (Matt. 5:44–45).

In response to the scholar's question about who our neighbor is, Jesus teaches the story of what is commonly called the Good Samaritan (Luke 10:30–37). Jews and Samaritans hated each other. Jews considered Samaritans half-breed Gentiles who had elements of pagan idolatry in their worship. Samaritans were an ethnic mixture of Gentile and Jew, as a result of the Assyrian exile of the Northern Tribes of Israel in 722 BC. Also in AD 6, a group of Samaritans desecrated the Jewish temple, widening the chasm between Samaritans and Jews even further. Racism, ethnocentrism, prejudice, bitterness, and religious bigotry created a strong wall of hate between them. As Jesus tells the story, the Jewish audience would have expected the Jewish priest or the Levite to help the Jewish man who was robbed and beaten nearly to death laying on the side of the road (Luke 10:31–32).

But the plot twist is that a Samaritan is the hero. The Samaritan man walked through the wall of racism and religious bigotry to give aid to a Jew, a person who was supposed to be his enemy (Luke 10:33–36). How did he do it? Maybe he saw himself in the barely alive Jewish man? Whatever it was, it brought compassion out of him.

It is compassion that breaks down the walls that divide us and builds bridges that unite us. Financially, the Samaritan provided oil, wine, bandages, and boarding at an inn, so the Jewish man could recover from the evil that befell him. Love means being generous to the poor, to people ethnically different than you, and even to your enemies.

IT IS COMPASSION THAT BREAKS DOWN THE WALLS THAT DIVIDE US AND BUILDS BRIDGES THAT UNITE US.

Loving people may not stop people from hating you, but it will stop you from hating them. When Jesus said to love your neighbor as yourself, he was summing up the kingdom of Abba for those who give their allegiance to him. Love that is divine, *agape*, God's-kind-of-love is not wimpy, weak, or sentimental. It is radical, revolutionary, and redemptive. Kingdom love is sacrificial and life-giving.

Justice Is Love on Public Display

Sometimes the pain of living in a not-yet-fully-redeemed world is too much to bear. Like you, I long for the wrongs to be made right, for hurts to be healed, for the forgotten to be remembered, for the oppressed to be treated with dignity, and for the untouchables to be held. We yearn for fairness for ourselves, do we not? I know we do because when we are treated unfairly, we let it be known. You and I cry out for justice.

According to the *Lexham Bible Dictionary*, justice (*mishpat*) is a "divinely righteous action, whether taken by God or humans, that promotes equality among humanity."[1] The kingdom of God is a kingdom of justice. And we, the sacred, Spirit-filled family of royal priests, are bringers of Abba's justice.

To love our neighbor as ourselves is simply justice on public display. In the book of Leviticus, this biblical justice is outlined in practical terms:

 THE KINGDOM OF GOD IS A KINGDOM OF JUSTICE.

> "When you reap the harvest of your land, you are not to reap to the very edge of your field or gather the gleanings of your harvest. Do not strip your vineyard bare or gather its fallen grapes. Leave

---

[1] J. K. Garrett, "Justice" in J. D. Barry, D. Bomar, D. R. Brown, R. Klippenstein, D. Mangum, C. Sinclair Wolcott, W. Widder, et al. (eds.), *Lexham Bible Dictionary* (Bellingham, WA: Lexham Press, 2016).

them for the poor and the resident alien; I am the
LORD your God.

"Do not steal. Do not act deceptively or lie to
one another. Do not swear falsely by my name,
profaning the name of your God; I am the LORD.

"Do not oppress your neighbor or rob him.
The wages due a hired worker must not remain
with you until morning. Do not curse the deaf or
put a stumbling block in front of the blind, but
you are to fear your God; I am the LORD.

"Do not act unjustly when deciding a case. Do
not be partial to the poor or give preference to the
rich; judge your neighbor fairly. Do not go about
spreading slander among your people; do not
jeopardize your neighbor's life; I am the LORD.

"Do not harbor hatred against your brother.
Rebuke your neighbor directly, and you will not
incur guilt because of him. Do not take revenge
or bear a grudge against members of your community, but love your neighbor as yourself; I am
the LORD." (Lev. 19:9–18)

Loving your neighbors as you love yourself means being generous to the poor. (Lev. 19:9-10)

In ancient times, the Jewish people were to leave produce for
the poor by not harvesting all the food from their fields. The food
left was for the poor to gather and eat, or glean. As a means of providing for the poor, Yahweh commanded his people to be generous.
Loving your neighbor through generosity is worship.

Singing songs to Abba is good, but if we do that without loving our neighbor, we're hypocrites. The apostle John said it is impossible to love God, who we can't see, if we don't love our neighbor, who we can see. Going through the motions of religion while failing to be generous to the poor is a horrible hypocrisy, and God's prophets regularly rebuked the nation of Israel for just that.

> I hate, I despise, your feasts!
> I can't stand the stench
> of your solemn assemblies.
> Even if you offer me
> your burnt offerings and grain offerings,
> I will not accept them;
> I will have no regard
> for your fellowship offerings of fattened cattle.
> Take away from me the noise of your songs!
> I will not listen to the music of your harps.
> But let justice flow like water,
> and righteousness, like an unfailing stream.
> (Amos 5:21–24)

When we sacrificially and joyfully give to the poor, we are giving a loan to Abba himself (Prov. 19:17). Sharing with those in need pleases the heart of God (Heb. 13:16). Abba, through his family of royal priests, executes his "justice for the exploited" and gives "food to the hungry" (Ps. 146:7).

Loving your neighbors as you love yourself means showing hospitality to people of different ethnicities. (Lev. 19:9–10)

As royal priests, we are given the privilege and responsibility of providing for the needs of the immigrant or "resident alien" (Lev. 19:10). God gives us the gift of loving people across ethnic barriers that the demonic realm has constructed to divide us. We are our brothers' and sisters' keepers. We are not to just look out for our own interests but the interests of others. There is no "us vs. them." There is only us.

THERE IS NO "US VS. THEM." THERE IS ONLY US.

Do nothing out of selfish ambition or conceit, but in humility consider others as more important than yourselves. Everyone should look not to his own interests, but rather to the interests of others. (Phil. 2:3–4)

Beneath our skin, we all look the same. Blood, guts, bones, ligaments, and soul. As in the story of the Good Samaritan above, your generosity to the poor and how you treat people of different ethnicities communicates your loyalty to Abba's kingdom.

Loving your neighbor as you love yourself means living a life of integrity. (Lev. 19:11)

We love our neighbors by living a life of integrity. This means we are truthful and trustworthy.

> For the LORD God is a sun and shield. The LORD grants favor and honor; he does not withhold the good from those who live with integrity. (Ps. 84:11)

Lying, stealing, bearing false witness, and failing to fulfill promises are incompatible with the gospel of Abba's kingdom. If you neglect walking in reliance on the Spirit's power, your moral compass will get broken and you will lose your way.

Loving your neighbor as you love yourself means promoting economic justice. (Lev. 19:12–13)

In the ancient world, like in our own, the poor, the powerless and the oppressed were taken advantage of economically. This behavior is sin. James, the half-brother of Jesus, writes these stinging words to Christians who were taking advantage of other Christians by not paying them what they were worth, even withholding their wages:

> Come now, you rich people, weep and wail over the miseries that are coming on you. Your wealth has rotted and your clothes are moth-eaten. Your gold and silver are corroded, and their corrosion will be a witness against you and will eat your flesh like fire. You have stored up treasure in the last days. Look! The pay that you withheld from

the workers who mowed your fields cries out, and
the outcry of the harvesters has reached the ears of
the Lord of Armies. (James 5:1–4)

How we treat the vulnerable, marginalized, and disenfranchised is a sign of our love for Jesus. Abba blesses us to be a blessing. We leverage our lives and influence on behalf of the other, especially the other who has been forgotten and left behind.

Loving your neighbor as you love yourself means caring for people with disabilities. (Lev. 19:14)

Ever since I was a little boy, I've had a tender spot in my heart for people with disabilities. If you want to make me lose it, just be rude or take advantage of a person with disabilities in my presence. I know I should not sin in my anger, and I hope I would be able in that context, but my heart is just bent toward protecting the vulnerable in this way.

Loving our neighbor means caring, protecting, and empowering our brothers and sisters with disabilities so they can flourish. As we pursue God's kingdom of love, we will show love to all members of humanity, including those who are physically, emotionally, or mentally disabled.

Loving your neighbor as you love yourself means promoting an equitable justice system. (Lev. 19:15-16)

There are often two justice systems in America and other places in the world. One for the wealthy and one for the poor. How is it that banks can admit fraud, pay a fine, and no one goes to prison, but a man who steals to eat is sent to jail until he can pay bail or have a trial? Here is an example:

> [Company X] has agreed to pay $3 billion to settle criminal charges and a civil action stemming from its widespread mistreatment of customers in its community bank over a 14-year period, the Justice Department announced on Friday. From 2002 to 2016, employees used fraud to meet impossible sales goals. They opened millions of accounts in customers' names without their knowledge, signed unwitting account holders up for credit cards and bill payment programs, created fake personal identification numbers, forged signatures and even secretly transferred customers' money.[2]

But prisons are filled with poor people who have committed lesser crimes, or who have not even been convicted of any crime, but just can't pay bail.

Similarly, prisons are brimming with people who have used or sold drugs, but multi-billion-dollar pharmaceutical companies can create addictive opioids, like OxyContin, pay $8 billion in fines, and not worry about prison time. The opioid crisis is killing Americans at an alarming rate. The biggest dope dealer is no longer on a street corner; his stock is publicly traded on the New York Stock Exchange.

---

[2] Emily Flitter, "The Price of Wells Fargo's Fake Account Scandal Grows by $3 Billion," February 21, 2020, https://www.nytimes.com/2020/02/21/business/wells-fargo-settlement.html (accessed November 8, 2020).

God, do you hear me?

The drugmaker blamed for helping to unleash America's staggering opioid crisis agreed to plead guilty to criminal charges as part of an $8 billion settlement over its marketing of OxyContin, the Department of Justice revealed Wednesday. The company agreed to pay the massive fines and admit criminal liability, but company executives and . . . do not admit to any criminal wrongdoing in the agreement.[3]

Are the families who have lost loved ones going to see any of the 8 billion dollars being paid to the government?

Love means caring about equality in the justice system. Equal for the rich and poor, the black, the Latino, the Asian, and the white, the male and female. If you do not speak up for the voiceless, who will? Love means speaking up for those who cannot.[4]

 LOVE MEANS SPEAKING UP FOR THOSE WHO CANNOT.

---

[3] Pete Williams, "OxyContin maker Purdue Pharma pleads guilty to federal criminal charges," October 21, 2020, https://www.nbcnews.com/news/us-news/oxycontin-drugmaker-purdue-pharma-pleads-guilty-federal-criminal-charges-n1244155 (accessed November 8, 2020).

[4] See the Equal Justice Initiative at https://eji.org/about/.

Loving your neighbor as you love yourself means pursuing a life of grace, compassion, mercy and forgiveness. (Lev. 19:17–19)

Loving your neighbor means treating all people the way Jesus has treated you. Jesus has treated you with grace, compassion, mercy, and forgiveness. The cycle of violence and vitriol is only undone by love. Drink deeply from the apostle's words:

> Live in harmony with each other. Don't be too proud to enjoy the company of ordinary people. And don't think you know it all!
>
> Never pay back evil with more evil. Do things in such a way that everyone can see you are honorable. Do all that you can to live in peace with everyone.
>
> Dear friends, never take revenge. Leave that to the righteous anger of God. For the Scriptures say,
>
> "I will take revenge;
> I will pay them back,"
> says the LORD.
>
> Instead,
> "If your enemies are hungry, feed them.
> If they are thirsty, give them something to drink.
> In doing this, you will heap
> burning coals of shame on their heads."
>
> Don't let evil conquer you, but conquer evil by doing good. (Rom. 12:16–21 NLT)

> Love does no wrong to others, so love fulfills the
> requirements of God's law. (Rom. 13:10 NLT)

This kind of love is beyond us. This is why Abba plants it in us. The only way we can love like this is to be close and intimate with love himself.

> Instead, clothe yourself with the presence of the
> Lord Jesus Christ. And don't let yourself think
> about ways to indulge your evil desires. (Rom.
> 13:14 NLT)

When we pray "your kingdom come . . . on earth as it is in heaven," we are asking God to help us love our neighbor. We are requesting to become a person that "does no wrong to a neighbor" (Rom. 13:10). As we pursue this kingdom of love with our lives, acting justly and generously, we are offering true and beautiful worship.

—————— Marinate on This ——————

Prayer

Abba,

Teach me, mold me by the Spirit,

into a person who loves my neighbor as myself.

Clothe me in Christ, every second of every day, so
I can love my neighbor and wrong no one.

Love is giving.

Love is living.

Love is fulfilling.

Love is sacrificial.

Love is patient beyond reason.

Love is hopeful when it makes no sense.

Love conquers evil.

Love defeats death.

Love rights the wrongs.

Love bottles every tear.

Love heals the hurt.

Love sets the captives free.

Love lifts the oppressed.

God, do you hear me?

Love humbles the proud.

Love gives grace to the humble.

Love welcomes all the prodigals home.

Love runs after the runways.

Love is forgiving and sin-killing.

Love looks like a bloody man on the cross.

Love looks like an empty tomb.

Love has a name. It is Jesus.

Fill me so his justice can be on display as I love my neighbor,

This is the kingdom of Abba.

Amen.

Questions for Reflection

1. We saw at the very beginning of this chapter that for Abba's kids, love and obedience go hand-in-hand. Is that how you're used to thinking about these two things? Is that the picture of Christianity that is often painted in the world?

2. Based on this chapter, how would you define biblical justice?

3. Is the command to "love your neighbor" abstract and vague, or concrete and specific, according to Scripture? How do you know?

4. Is there any area in your life where you need to repent for failing to love your neighbor well? How is the Holy Spirit working in you now to be an ambassador of God's kingdom justice?

Points to Remember

1. "The one who does not love does not know God, because God is love" (1 John 4:8).

2. Love has a name—Jesus.

3. We are our brothers' and sisters' keepers. We are not to just look out for our own interests but the interests of others. There is no "us vs. them." There is only us.

4. Loving your neighbor means treating all people the way Jesus has treated you. Jesus has treated you with grace, compassion, mercy, and forgiveness. The cycle of violence and vitriol is only undone by love.

Depending on the Bread of Life

"Give us today our daily bread."
MATTHEW 6:11

As the Bread of Life, Jesus is our provider, our breadwinner. He alone sustains us with his being. Jesus cares about the whole of our lives, not just our souls. He graciously meets our every need, at every level of our being.

> And my God will supply all your needs according to his riches in glory in Christ Jesus. Now to our God and Father be glory forever and ever. Amen. (Phil. 4:19–20)

CHAPTER 11

Soul Food from Heaven

My hope for you and me as we journey together through the pages of this book is that we will embrace the reality that Jesus is the Bread of Life. He is the *soul food* from heaven that supplies our every need:

> Jesus said to them, "Truly I tell you, Moses didn't give you the bread from heaven, but my Father gives you the true bread from heaven. For the bread of God is the one who comes down from heaven and gives life to the world." Then they said, "Sir, give us this bread always." "I am the bread of life," Jesus told them. (John 6:32–35)
>
> And my God will supply all your needs according to his riches in glory in Christ Jesus. Now to our God and Father be glory forever and ever. Amen. (Phil. 4:19–20)

He is our provider.

He is our breadwinner, equipped with an inexhaustible work ethic on our behalf.

He is the one who sustains us with his divine being.

He is the one who cares about the whole of our lives—body and soul.

He is the one who heals our diseases and is the cure for our death.

He is the one who provides where he guides.

He is the one who meets our needs, not our greeds.

Ultimately, as we look back over the horizon of our lives, we will be happy that he did not give us our greeds. In his infinite knowledge and grace, Abba does not answer our selfish, misdirected prayers. If he gave us everything we prayed for, we would begin to worship the things he gives us, instead of him! This type of worship is idolatry, and it ruins us to the core. Jesus loves us too much to ruin us with too much. Our overabundance meets someone else's needs.

IF GOD GAVE US EVERYTHING WE PRAYED FOR, WE WOULD BEGIN TO WORSHIP THE THINGS HE GIVES US, INSTEAD OF HIM!

It is not that there should be relief for others and hardship for you, but it is a question of equality. At the present time your surplus is available for their need, so that their abundance may in turn meet your need, in order that there may be equality. As it is written: The person who had much did not have too much, and the person who had little did not have too little. (2 Cor. 8:13–15)

The Question

Here is a question I want you to marinate on.

It is a question that can change your understanding of prayer, why you pray, and how you pray. It is a question that can renovate your life:

> If God answered all of your prayers, would your life become more *holy*?

When I say holy, I mean what the apostle Paul meant when he wrote this to the multiethnic churches in Colossae,

> Therefore, as God's chosen ones, holy and dearly loved, put on compassion, kindness, humility, gentleness, and patience, bearing with one another and forgiving one another if anyone has a grievance against another. Just as the Lord has forgiven you, so you are also to forgive. Above all, put on love, which is the perfect bond of unity. And let the peace of Christ, to which you were also called in one body, rule your hearts. And be thankful. Let the word of Christ dwell richly among you, in all wisdom teaching and admonishing one another through psalms, hymns, and spiritual songs, singing to God with gratitude in your hearts. And whatever you do, in word or in deed, do everything in the name of the Lord Jesus, giving thanks to God the Father through him. (Col. 3:12–17)

A holy life, as Paul describes, is a life that has been captivated and motivated by the grace of Abba in Christ, through the Spirit. It is a life engulfed and animated by the character of the triune God. A holy life is a life that is consciously living in and from the finished work of King Jesus. Jesus, the true human, came on a mission to reverse the curse of Adam and to make humanity great again.

> If by the one man's trespass, death reigned through that one man, how much more will those who receive the overflow of grace and the gift of righteousness reign in life through the one man, Jesus Christ. (Rom. 5:17)

The Recorder

If you were to record your prayers, I suspect, based on nearly twenty-five years of ministry, that 70 to 80 percent of your prayers would be asking God to meet your needs, heal sick friends, help your kids do well in school, pay bills, get a better job and make more money, lose weight or get in better shape, have safety in travel, or avoid suffering or persecution.

Is anything wrong with these prayers? No, there is nothing wrong with those prayers in and of themselves. But when these prayers *permeate* and *dominate* your prayer life, instead of your prayer being about Jesus permeating and *shaping* your life to reflect Abba's kingdom, things get disordered and out of whack. The subtle shift, from praying for *stuff* to praying primarily for the inbreaking of the kingdom into your life, can transform your prayers.

I am about to give you some strong medicine. At first, it is going to taste really nasty. But it is good for you. I promise. I have taken this medicine, too. I just had a swig before I started writing this chapter.

Often, our prayers are like visiting Jesus for Thanksgiving dinner. We walk into his house with dirty shoes on, leaving mud tracks. We sit down at his table hardly acknowledging his presence. We pile so much food on our plates it looks like a mountain with an avalanche of gravy sliding down, dripping onto the table. And we eat his delicious food without hardly saying a word to him. He tries to talk to us, but we keep interrupting him with a request to pass the cranberry sauce.

It never dawns on us that Thanksgiving dinner is not about the food.

Thanksgiving dinner is about the One who made us thankful by dying on a cross in our place to give us grace and a space in his family. We find ourselves at Thanksgiving dinner with Jesus just to eat his food, not meet with him and enjoy him. As we stuff our faces, he looks at us, longing for conversation and communion. Instead, when we do look up from our plates, we ask him, "Is there more gravy? What's for dessert?"

We stuff our bellies like we are at a feeding trough. Then we get up to leave. As we are walking past him on the way out, we say, "That was great. What an incredible Thanksgiving. And Jesus, there are some things I need you to do for me and get me. When can I send you my Christmas list? Love ya, mean it."

Abba in Christ Jesus longs for us to know him and want him more than anything else in the world. Why? Is it because Abba is needy or insecure? No—it is because he loves you and wants what is best for you. What is best for you is him. What good is it if our needs are met, but we are not transformed by Jesus' loving presence into kingdom-of-Abba-kind-of-people?

WHAT GOOD IS IT IF OUR NEEDS ARE MET, BUT WE ARE NOT TRANSFORMED BY JESUS' LOVING PRESENCE INTO KINGDOM-OF-ABBA-KIND-OF-PEOPLE?

"For what does it benefit someone to gain the whole world and yet lose his life?" (Mark 8:36)

Asking Jesus to meet our needs without him meeting our greatest need is like dressing a scarecrow in the finest clothes and feeding it the best food. The provision is wasted and unappreciated. When we pray for God to give us God, for him to align us to his will, his provision becomes a means of worship. It also provides us with resources to live out our royal priesthood calling in the world. Abba wants us to long for him so we will not worship his provision, but him, the provider. The apostle Paul expresses this Jesus-centered perspective saying,

> I also consider everything to be a loss in view of the surpassing value of knowing Christ Jesus my Lord. (Phil. 3:8)

Abba Knows

Parents have a way of knowing what their children's needs are, often before the children do. Especially moms. Mommas have a built-in sensory system that alerts them to their kids' needs.

As our kids got older, some of my wife's sensory skills rubbed off on me. I developed a fatherly intuition to discern Presley and Jeremiah's needs. Vicki and I knew, not perfectly, but consistently, what our children needed. We could anticipate their needs because we loved and knew them better than they knew themselves.

If you and I, as fallible humans, can anticipate our children's needs, how much more can our infallible Abba, who knew us before we were born, know our needs? Abba does not merely anticipate our needs, following an intuition and making a best guess that usually turns out right. *He eternally knows our needs.* If this is true, and it is, why do we allow so much of our prayers to be a wish list instead of listening to God? Sit in the wisdom of these ancient words,

> My son, if you accept my words and store up my commands within you, listening closely to wisdom and directing your heart to understanding; furthermore, if you call out to insight and lift your voice to understanding, if you seek it like silver and search for it like hidden treasure, then you will understand the fear of the LORD and discover the knowledge of God. For the LORD gives wisdom; from his mouth come knowledge and understanding. (Prov. 2:1–6)

Why do we spend so much time asking God for things instead of asking for God himself?

> As a deer longs for flowing streams, so I long for you, God. I thirst for God, the living God. (Ps. 42:1–2)

Abba already knows what your needs are, and he promises to meet those needs. Listen to Jesus,

"So don't worry, saying, 'What will we eat?' or 'What will we drink?' or 'What will we wear?' For the Gentiles eagerly seek all these things, and your heavenly Father knows that you need them. But seek first the kingdom of God and his righteousness, and all these things will be provided for you. Therefore don't worry about tomorrow, because tomorrow will worry about itself. Each day has enough trouble of its own." (Matt. 6:31–34)

 ABBA ALREADY KNOWS WHAT YOUR NEEDS ARE, AND HE PROMISES TO MEET THOSE NEEDS.

Abba knows that your mortgage is due.

Abba knows you need a job.

Abba knows you need to eat and drink water to live.

Abba knows you need clothes to wear.

Abba knows. He is not distant. He is not hard of hearing. He is not aloof. He is near. He loves you.

Why do we worry about God meeting our needs so much when he said he would? And what can cure us of this constant worry? The cure for *worry* is *worship*.

Abba > Things

I have more than fifteen tailor-made suits in my closet. These suits are a testimony of God's grace, but not in the way you think.

I grew up poor. I shopped at the store called Hand-Me-Downs. This means that when my big cousin got to be too big for his clothes, he handed them down to me. Sometimes kids would laugh at me because of my clothes. I told myself that when I got some money, I was going to wear nice suits so no one could ever make fun of me again. When I made it to the NFL, my suit collection began. I had a tailor from Washington, DC, fly to Indianapolis to make suits for me. When I put on those suits, I felt good about myself. I felt like I had made it. I bought into the mantra, "The suit makes the man."

Unsurprisingly, after a few years of acquiring suits, the newness wore off, and the pain I was hoping my outer clothing could heal snuck back up to the surface. In fact, the pain was worse because I had worked so hard to become financially successful in order to get rid of the pain.

The things I wanted—the Lexus, the house, the clothes, all the things American culture told me meant I was successful—could not heal my deepest hurts. It was not until Abba gave me the clothes I was truly made for that healing began to happen.

> For those of you who were baptized into Christ
> have been clothed with Christ. (Gal. 3:27)

What Abba clothed me with on the inside was greater than what I was clothed with on the outside.

Our Western, consumeristic culture conditions us toward materialism. We believe that stuff will fulfill us. Instead of seeking God first, we pursue stuff first. When we dislodge ourselves from God's story, we ask God to fit into our story. Our story would read, "Seek first an SUV, a nice house in the suburbs or a dope condo in a gentrified urban area, designer clothes, financial security, and all the food we like."

OUR WESTERN, CONSUMERISTIC CULTURE CONDITIONS US TOWARD MATERIALISM. WE BELIEVE THAT STUFF WILL FULFILL US. INSTEAD OF SEEKING GOD FIRST, WE PURSUE STUFF FIRST.

Like you, I feel this tug every single day to ask God for stuff instead of delighting in Jesus and trusting him to provide for my needs.

College tuition is expensive.

Home repairs are expensive.

Medical care is expensive.

But if Jesus commands us to seek Abba's kingdom and righteousness first, he will provide for our needs. If God commands it, he will give us the grace to do it. Yet, we must participate in that grace by faith. Faith is simply saying, "Jesus, I am hanging on to you and not letting go."

Jesus gives us a marvelous guarantee in Matthew 6:33. Paraphrasing his words, it says "Precious child of Abba, you ask for so little. You have been blood-bought by me to share in my glory. Because you are 'in me,' you are a royal priest, created by grace to be my coheir in Abba's kingdom. You are praying for trinkets, and Abba wants to give you something greater—himself—so you can live out his righteousness in an unrighteous world. The prayers for stuff that dominate your mind and cause anxiety will never satisfy you. Desire Abba's kingdom and righteousness above all. Do not sweat the small stuff. I got you. You can trust me. I am not going to send you on a mission without the proper provisions."

Finding Our Hearts' True Treasure

When we pray, "Give us today our daily bread" (Matt. 6:11), we are making a declaration of worship. We are saying, "Today, we trust you, Abba, to provide for us through Christ Jesus." Worship is telling God in prayer, "Jesus is the Bread of Life. I do not have to worry about him meeting my needs because he is faithful to do so. Therefore, I will spend my time captivated by his grace and pursuing his kingdom. He will feed and clothe me for the mission."

WHEN WE PRAY, "GIVE US TODAY OUR DAILY BREAD" (MATT. 6:11), WE ARE MAKING A DECLARATION OF WORSHIP. WE ARE SAYING, "TODAY, WE TRUST YOU, ABBA, TO PROVIDE FOR US THROUGH CHRIST JESUS."

When I was a little boy, I believed every word my grandmother told me. During the late 1970s, when Bigfoot was all the rage, she told me that Bigfoot came to our backyard every night. I ran to the backyard and found some big footprints. Wow! Who would have thought Bigfoot was coming to my backyard. Of course, the footprints belonged to my grandmother, but it was super fun believing Bigfoot visited the ghetto.

Another time, she told me that there was a buried treasure in our backyard. I was obsessed with finding it. After bugging her day after day, she finally told me where the treasure was, and I started digging. And digging. And digging. I kept digging because my heart was committed to finding the treasure.

Persistence in prayer is vital. As a father, I love when my children come to me for advice, for encouragement, and provision. My wife and I have worked hard to meet Presley and Jeremiah's needs, physically, emotionally, and spiritually. Abba delights in meeting our needs. Abba delights in us calling his name. Abba never grows weary of hearing our prayers. As we pray more, we grow nearer to him and his heart for us. Prayer bonds us to him.

Just as my kids come to me with boldness, we can come to Abba with bold prayers (Luke 11:8). He is our Father, our Creator, and he is good. He wants us to, "ask, and it will be given to you. Seek, and you will find. Knock, and the door will be opened to you" (Luke 11:9). If my daughter asks me for something to eat, I am not going to give her a rock, as her father, because I love her, I'm going to get her something to eat. How much more true is this of our Abba.

> "What father among you, if his son asks for a fish, will give him a snake instead of a fish? Or if he asks for an egg, will give him a scorpion? If you then, who are evil, know how to give good gifts to your children, how much more will the heavenly Father give the Holy Spirit to those who ask him?" (Luke 11:11–13)

As we pray with boldness, not only do we have our physical needs met, God the Holy Spirit meets our spiritual needs so we can discern the heart and will of Abba in our lives.

When we pray, "Give us today our daily bread," we are declaring that Jesus himself is the greatest treasure, not stuff. Are clothes, cars, homes, and money important? Yes. But without Jesus living in us and through us and us treasuring him above all, the stuff is empty. I join with the apostle Paul in declaring the "incalculable riches of Christ" (Eph. 3:8), the "riches of his grace" (Eph. 1:7), and "the riches of his glorious inheritance" (Eph. 1:18 NIV), he is the greatest treasure. We treasure him above all because,

> For you know the grace of our Lord Jesus Christ: Though he was rich, for your sake he became poor, so that by his poverty you might become rich. (2 Cor. 8:9)

King Jesus, the praise of all of heaven, steps into time and space to pour the riches of his grace upon us. We go from spiritual poverty to endless riches in his kingdom. The riches are not stuff. He is the treasure. As we treasure him, our hearts will trust him to provide for our needs. Jesus says,

> "Don't store up for yourselves treasures on earth, where moth and rust destroy and where thieves break in and steal. But store up for yourselves treasures in heaven, where neither moth nor rust destroys, and where thieves don't break in and steal. For where your treasure is, there your heart will be also." (Matt. 6:19–21)

May our hearts forever rest in the nail-pierced hands of the Bread of Life, our provider.

─────────── Marinate on This ───────────

Prayer

Abba,

Give me an appetite for the Bread of Life.

May my hunger pains only be filled by him.

Give me the courage to seek first your kingdom and righteousness.

Spirit,

Give me the faith to trust that Jesus will
provide for my every need.

Give me the discernment to know the
difference between a need and a greed.

When I worry, give me a heart of worship.

King Jesus,

Remind me every day that you are the great treasure.

Remind me every day of the riches of your
grace and glory and kingdom.

Remind me that only you satisfy.

"Blessed are those who hunger and thirst for
righteousness, for they will be filled" (Matt. 5:6).

In Jesus' name, amen.

Questions for Reflection

1. Did Pastor Derwin's illustration about Thanksgiving dinner seem reminiscent of your prayer life at all? Why or why not?

2. How has the desire for stuff shown itself in your life?

3. What are the things that, if you're honest, you've always thought will help rid you of pain, or that empty feeling inside?

4. How does the truth that God eternally knows everything you need—and has the loving heart of a Father to meet your needs—change the way you think about prayer?

Things to Remember

1. In his infinite knowledge and grace, Abba does not answer our selfish, misdirected prayers. If he gave us everything we prayed for, we would begin to worship the things he gives us, instead of him!

2. Our Western, consumeristic culture conditions us toward materialism. We believe that stuff will fulfill us. Instead of seeking God first, we pursue stuff first.

3. When we pray, "Give us today our daily bread," we are declaring that Jesus himself is the greatest treasure, not stuff.

4. King Jesus, the praise of all of heaven, steps into time and space to pour the riches of his grace upon us. We go from spiritual poverty to endless riches in his kingdom. The riches are not stuff. He is the treasure.

CHAPTER 12

Worship > Worry

Nothing is out of reach for Abba's sovereign hand of love that draws us into his redemptive purpose. Often the seeds planted deep in the soil in our souls take years to grow and produce a harvest. One such moment for me began in 1987 when I was a sophomore at Converse Judson High School in a bedroom community of San Antonio, Texas. I had just transferred to Judson from Fox Tech, an inner-city school. I was leaving the familiar, both culturally and ethnically. I had never gone to school with white kids, but it was time for me to transfer after a year in Judson's school district. I was tired of waking up at 5:30 a.m., walking a mile and a half to the bus stop, and then being on the bus for an hour to make it to school in the city on time. Also, I knew that if I wanted to play college football, I needed to transfer to Judson. Judson was a state power in football under legendary coach D. W. Rutledge.

In the offseason, Coach Rutledge and the staff took the football team through a week-long training called "The Classroom" to prepare us for life on and off the field. In one class, Coach Rutledge said, "I can guarantee that you can become a millionaire by the time you are sixty-five years old." Immediately, like after drinking a strong cup of Dominican coffee, I was alert to every word that came out of his mouth.

Coach Rutledge began to teach us the power of compound interest and the Rule of 72 in investing. The Rule of 72 estimates how your investment will increase over time. When you know the rate of return on an investment, the Rule of 72 will tell how many years it will take for your investment to double in value. Coach Rutledge taught us to divide the number 72 by our investment's expected rate of return. I looked on in amazement. I could become a millionaire if I did what he said.

Then he told us, "Every day that you work hard in the classroom and in your athletic training, you are making an investment in your life, and the compound interest will grow you into a person and player that can make a positive difference in the world."

That illustration changed my life.

I had found the treasure that my sixteen-year-old heart was looking for.

If I worked hard, I could go to college and make something of myself.

I did not let anything get in the way of this treasure I had found.

With relentless attention to detail and a work ethic to match, my heart found the treasure. Ultimately, I played college football and then became an NFL player. But my heart thought football was the treasure. It was not. Football was just the road that led me home to Abba's house. Jesus opened the door for me and let me in. The real treasure was the Father, the Son, and the Spirit.

MY HEART THOUGHT FOOTBALL WAS THE TREASURE. IT WAS NOT. FOOTBALL WAS JUST THE ROAD THAT LED ME HOME TO ABBA'S HOUSE.

Better Investment Than the Stock Market

Jesus says, "For where your treasure is, there your heart will be also" (Matt. 6:21). When you come to the place where Jesus is your greatest treasure, he will have your heart. When this happens, you will desire to invest all of who you are—your talent, treasure, and time—in his kingdom. You will want to sell everything because you have found where you belong, and the longings of your heart are satisfied in him.

> "The kingdom of heaven is like treasure, buried in a field, that a man found and reburied. Then in his joy he goes and sells everything he has and buys that field." (Matt. 13:44)

Jesus and his "incalculable riches" are the treasure of unending and unmeasurable worth (Eph. 3:8). He lives in those who call on his name.

> Now we have this treasure in clay jars, so that this extraordinary power may be from God and not from us. (2 Cor. 4:7)

One of the ways we praise Jesus for the riches of his grace is to trust him to provide for our needs. If Abba in Christ, by the Spirit, can defeat sin, death, and evil on your behalf, then providing for your needs is easy. When we pray, "Give us today our daily bread," we are saying, "Jesus, we are choosing to worship instead of worry."

ONE OF THE WAYS WE PRAISE JESUS FOR THE RICHES OF HIS GRACE IS TO TRUST HIM TO PROVIDE FOR OUR NEEDS.

The Healthy Eye and the Bad Eye

Jesus knew the utter decadence of the Roman elite. In first-century Roman culture, status was an idol, just like today. One of the ways the Roman elite showed their status was by having banquets where guests would try to eat themselves into oblivion. They would gorge themselves with food and drink while laying sideways so their stomachs would not get too full. But when their stomach did get full, they would vomit at the table to create more room so they could eat and drink more. It was an epic display of gluttony, which is a sin.

> Their end is destruction; their god is their stomach; their glory is in their shame; and they are focused on earthly things. (Phil. 3:19)

On the other end of the spectrum, the poor, whether Jew or Gentile, lived in a much different world.

Food and water were scarce.

Living conditions were cramped.

Fifty percent of children died at birth or during infancy.[1]

Cities were filled with racial hatred.

Disease was everywhere.

---

[1] Rodney Stark, *The Rise of Christianity* (New York: Harper One, 1996), 160.

Life expectancy was short.

Life was hard for the poor in the ancient world, not unlike today.

It is in this world of extreme poverty and extreme wealth that Jesus said,

> "The eye is the lamp of the body. If your eye is healthy, your whole body will be full of light. But if your eye is bad, your whole body will be full of darkness. So if the light within you is darkness, how deep is that darkness!" (Matt. 6:22–23)

Jesus uses a common metaphor about eyes to help us trust that God will provide for our needs. The better our eyes, the clearer we see. The better our spiritual eyes, the clearer we see reality from God's vantage point.

In Matthew 6:22–23, Jesus' illustration about a healthy eye and a bad eye made sense to his first-century Jewish audience. The healthy eye meant looking upon others with a heart of generosity because they were looking to Abba with single-minded devotion.[2] The person with a bad eye was a person with a heart trapped in comparison, jealousy, competition, greed, and stinginess.[3]

A person with a bad eye has a scarcity mentality. A person with a good eye has a generosity mentality.

Never forget this—lock and tuck this gospel-truth away in your heart: Worship is better than comparison. Worship leads to the light and comparison leads to the darkness. Nothing good comes from being in darkness.

---

[2] Stark, 160.
[3] Stark, 160.

Jesus, the Bread of Life, the Light of the World, came on a mission to open our eyes and free us from the dungeon of darkness. When we look to food, drink, and clothes, or any other created thing to satisfy us, we walk into a dark dungeon of idolatry.

JESUS, THE BREAD OF LIFE, THE LIGHT OF THE WORLD, CAME ON A MISSION TO OPEN OUR EYES AND FREE US FROM THE DUNGEON OF DARKNESS.

There is nothing good there.

Nothing.

Even good things become bad things in this place. That's why Jesus came:

> "In order to open blind eyes,
> to bring out prisoners from the dungeon,
> and those sitting in darkness from the prison
>   house."
> (Isa. 42:7)

On the other hand, when we look to Abba to satisfy us, we walk in the bright and beautiful light of generosity. When we know food, drink, clothes, and money cannot satisfy us or save us, we hold onto them with a loose hand, and we give them freely to those who need them most.

Comparison Dissolves Trust in Abba

One of the fastest ways to get discouraged is to compare what we have with what someone else has. My wife taught me: "We often compare our insides with someone else's outsides." What God has for you, he has for *you*. His provision for someone else is not going to fit you anyway. When we look at what others have, the dark powers whisper into our hearts, "You see, if God really loved you, you would have more money, you would eat better, you would have better clothes, you would have a better house. Why do other people get blessings, but you don't?" Comparison *dissolves* our trust in Abba.

Whenever doubt about Abba's faithfulness to provide for us creeps in—and it will—remember that he provided his Son for us on a cross. If Abba gave up his Son to redeem us, he is able to meet our needs.

 WE OFTEN COMPARE OUR INSIDES WITH SOMEONE ELSE'S OUTSIDES.

He did not even spare his own Son but gave him up for us all. (Rom. 8:32)

Comparison Detaches Us from Gratitude

When we compare what we have with what others have, we *detach* ourselves from having a heart of gratitude. It is impossible to appreciate what you have when your eyes are lusting for what others have. A heart of gratitude is like having a horse blinder on. Horse blinders are leather squares that are affixed to a horse's bridle to prevent the horse from seeing behind and beside her as she pulls a wagon. The horse blinders keep the horse from being distracted by what is around them.

IT IS IMPOSSIBLE TO APPRECIATE WHAT YOU HAVE WHEN YOUR EYES ARE LUSTING FOR WHAT OTHERS HAVE.

Jesus does not blind us to keep us from being distracted.

Jesus opens our eyes so we can gaze upon his light of salvation.

Jesus enlightens our hearts so we can see the wealth of our eternal inheritance and his mighty power can be experienced.

> I pray that the eyes of your heart may be enlightened so that you may know what is the hope of his calling, what is the wealth of his glorious inheritance in the saints, and what is the immeasurable greatness of his power toward us who believe, according to the mighty working of his strength. (Eph. 1:18–19)

Comparison Destroys Contentment

During my second year in the NFL, I always felt like I had to buy something new to feel good. It was like there was always background noise in my mind telling me that I needed more to validate that I had become successful. My unsatisfied desire for more was a belly that could never be filled. Contentment became a rumor that I heard about but did not experience.

When we compare, we look at the things in our life through glasses that are tinted by envy. Everything looks worse and even things that once satisfied us can be transformed to cause us to want more or different things.

But God calls us to godliness and contentment:

> But godliness with contentment is great gain. For
> we brought nothing into the world, and we can
> take nothing out. If we have food and clothing,
> we will be content with these. (1 Tim. 6:6–8)

When we realize Abba has given us his Son, who is the Bread of Life, we rest in the knowledge that we have everything we need. Comparison destroys contentment; resting in Abba frees us from want and worry to be content.

Comparison Determines That Everyone Is Your Competition

Comparison *determines* that everyone is your competition. When everyone is your competition, you cannot celebrate the good gifts Abba blesses them with. When you see people as your competition, you think their blessing should have been yours. Envy, jealousy, and bitterness mark your life. No matter how successful you become or how much you have, it will never be enough. Not only will you become stingy with money, but you will also be stingy with encouragement.

A competitive spirit is always followed closely by an unwelcomed guest called discontentment. Instead of people being valued because they are made in the image of Abba, people become stepping stones to further your career opportunities. Instead of people being valued because Jesus died for them, you look for what you can get out of people, instead of how you can bless them.

You will become a taker instead of a giver.

You will look to be served instead of looking to serve.

You will become entitled instead of grateful.

> Do nothing out of selfish ambition or conceit, but in humility consider others as more important than yourselves. Everyone should look not to his own interests, but rather to the interests of others. (Phil. 2:3–4)

Comparison Draws Us Toward Greed

Greed is not just an upper-middle-class or rich person idol. Greed does not have anything to do with how much you have or do not have. Greed is about wanting more of something because you think that something will satisfy you more than Jesus. Comparison draws us toward greed. Jesus says,

> "No one can serve two masters, since either he will hate one and love the other, or he will be devoted to one and despise the other. You cannot serve both God and money." (Matt. 6:24)

GREED IS ABOUT WANTING MORE OF SOMETHING BECAUSE YOU THINK THAT SOMETHING WILL SATISFY YOU MORE THAN JESUS.

In this Scripture, Jesus teaches us that we will either have him or money as our master. In this first-century context of Jesus, a master meant the person you have given your allegiance to. Jesus redeems you with his blood (1 Cor. 6:19–20). Jesus' mastery of us leads to true freedom.

We are free to love God and our neighbors.

We are free from believing that money will satisfy us.

We are free to use money instead of being used by money.

The word Jesus used for money is *mammon*, which refers to all a person's material possessions and resources.[4] Here is where dark powers get a meat hook in our souls. As Americans, even amid the two recessions since 2008, we are still a prosperous nation. The wealthier a nation gets, the fewer people in that nation are dependent on Abba. America is swimming in materialism and consumerism. These worldviews tell us that we are what we have.

Ultimately, a choice must be made. Will I serve Jesus or will I trust *mammon*?

Here is the beauty of Abba's kingdom: *mammon* becomes good gifts that meet our needs and are stewarded to meet the needs of our brothers and sisters. When Jesus is our master, we learn to master *mammon*, instead of being mastered by it.

The Cure for Greed

The cure for greed is grace. As the Spirit of God penetrates our hearts, and as we allow his work of grace to take root by faith, we become generous. The apostle Paul had two main objectives in his missionary journeys: (1) plant multiethnic churches in fulfillment of the Abrahamic covenant and (2) raise financial support for the poor mother church in Jerusalem.

---

[4] Craig Blomberg, *Matthew, Vol. 22,* New American Commentary (Nashville: Broadman & Holman Publishers, 1992), 124.

THE CURE FOR GREED
IS GRACE.

By reading this you are able to understand my insight into the mystery of Christ. This was not made known to people in other generations as it is now revealed to his holy apostles and prophets by the Spirit: The Gentiles are coheirs, members of the same body, and partners in the promise in Christ Jesus through the gospel. (Eph. 3:4–6)

For I hope to see you when I pass through and to be assisted by you for my journey there, once I have first enjoyed your company for a while. Right now I am traveling to Jerusalem to serve the saints, because Macedonia and Achaia were pleased to make a contribution for the poor among the saints in Jerusalem. Yes, they were pleased, and indeed are indebted to them. For if the Gentiles have shared in their spiritual benefits, then they are obligated to minister to them in material needs. (Rom. 15:24–27)

As Paul raised money for the church in Jerusalem, he reminded the multiethnic churches in Corinth that financial giving is an act of grace (2 Cor. 8:7–9), that giving is a test of the genuineness of love (2 Cor. 8:8), and that our financial giving to the kingdom of God is a faithful response to Abba's grace in Christ to us (2 Cor. 8:9). Paul is saying that when you experience God's grace, when you remember the dark place he rescued you from, and when you think of his mercy and the newness of life in his kingdom, giving financially to the kingdom of God is a joyful response. It is an act of worship.

At the first of the month, an automatic withdrawal from our checking account goes to the church so others can experience God's grace. Every year, Vicki and I pray about what percentage of our income we will give for the gospel's sake. The tithe or 10% is the starting point. Every year, we pray to give above 10% of our income to Transformation Church and other ministries. Why? Because we know the grace of the Lord Jesus. The King stepped out of heaven into time and space to give me a place in his family.

I am redeemed.

I am regenerated.

I am forgiven.

I am righteous.

I am reconciled.

I am the dwelling place of the Spirit.

I am his. He is mine.

I am in Christ.

I am a member of the family Abba promised Abraham.

I have been written into God's story of redeeming grace.

After all Abba has done for me in Christ, how can I not be financially generous in funding his kingdom mission? Start being generous to your local church today.

Don't Worry about Your Life

It seems so foreign to our everyday experience not to worry. Yet Jesus says,

"Therefore I tell you: Don't worry about your life, what you will eat or what you will drink; or about your body, what you will wear. Isn't life more than food and the body more than clothing?" (Matt. 6:25)

What does he mean?

Jesus means that you can eat the best food, drink the best wine, wear the best clothes, and still be *dislocated* from Abba's love, *discontent* in what you have, and driven toward idolatry.

Life is more than the possession of things.

Jesus says to look at the birds and the beautiful wildflowers. If God cares for them, will he not care for you? Birds and flowers are not made in his image, but you are (Matt. 6:26–29). The only thing worry does is suck the energy out of today and distract us from God's promises.

Worry adds nothing to our lives, but worship does.

As you grow in worship, you grow in faith.

The cure for worry is worship.

THE ONLY THING WORRY DOES IS SUCK THE ENERGY OUT OF TODAY AND DISTRACT US FROM GOD'S PROMISES.

Worship is telling Jesus, at the gut level, "In light of your death and resurrection, I have burned the ships! I am not returning to the land that you freed me from by your blood. I am all in for you and your kingdom. I will not worry about what I will eat, or drink, or wear, because you already know my needs, and I trust you to provide for me as I partner with you in your kingdom."

When you pray, "Give us today our daily bread," you are saying, "Jesus, I trust you. I will take care of your kingdom business and you will take care of mine."

> "So don't worry, saying, 'What will we eat?' or 'What will we drink?' or 'What will we wear?' For the Gentiles eagerly seek all these things, and your heavenly Father knows that you need them. But seek first the kingdom of God, and his righteousness, and all these things will be provided for you. Therefore don't worry about tomorrow, because tomorrow will worry about itself. Each day has enough trouble of its own." (Matt. 6:31–34)

——————— Marinate on This ———————

Prayer

Abba,

If you gave up your Son to redeem me

If you gave me the Holy Spirit to seal me

And your love fills me

Why should I worry about what I will eat, drink, or wear?

Your faithful and trustworthy love, the cross,
and the empty tomb forever prove it.

Holy Spirit,

Give me a healthy eye so I can be generous.

There is no lack or scarcity in the kingdom.

Therefore, I can be generous because I know the grace
of King Jesus, though he was rich he became poor for
my sake that I might become rich in his grace.

Lord Jesus,

Give me a heart filled with your strength and single-
minded devotion to seek first Abba's kingdom and
his righteousness. May my life be characterized by the
fragrance of worship and not the stench of worry.

In Your name, amen.

Questions for Reflection

1. Derwin's wife, Vicki, taught him that we often compare our insides with other people's outsides. How have you found yourself doing that?

2. Why is it so natural for us to compare ourselves to others, and so hard to avoid doing so?

3. How have you seen the negative fruits of comparison—like discontentment and competition—in your life?

4. When you think of the people you admire most, do they seem like people who spend a lot of time comparing themselves to others? How can you see people like this as models in Jesus's school of prayer to help you grow as a disciple?

Things to Remember

1. One of the ways we praise Jesus for the riches of his grace is to trust him to provide for our needs.

2. It is impossible to appreciate what you have when your eyes are lusting for what others have.

3. Ultimately, a choice must be made. Will I serve Jesus or will I trust mammon?

Diving into God's Forgiveness

*"And forgive us our debts, as we also
have forgiven our debtors."*
MATTHEW 6:12

In this section, we will discover the life-giving forgiveness of Abba that is in Christ, and we will learn how to forgive those who have hurt us. In learning to receive Abba's forgiveness, we will see the uniqueness of Jesus. In learning how to forgive, we will see the humanity of those who have offended us. The cost of unforgiveness is too great to pay.

CHAPTER 13

How Can I Forgive?

There is something powerful about these three words from a father, "I love you." As one birthday became the next, and into my teenage years and later my twenties, I was on a quest to hear, "Son, I love you."

If you asked me at seventeen if that was what I wanted, I would have said, "No," because I did not have the emotional capacity to deal with my father-wound then. A physical wound left untreated turns into an infection that spreads throughout your body. An untreated soul-wound does the same. Often the most toxic people are people with untreated soul-wounds.

My father and I were close when he and my mom were together, but after my sixth birthday, we grew apart. My dad struggled with substance abuse. At fifty years old, I now know that so many substance use disorders are self-medication by a person suffering brain (mental) illness. Growing up in "the hood," brain illness was perceived as weakness. Instead of going to a psychiatrist for brain health medication, people would go to the liquor store or to the corner dope boy to quiet the feelings running wild in their minds. Instead of going to a therapist to talk through their problems, they talked with others in the grips of untreated disorders. Instead of going to a treatment facility for help, they committed crimes to feed a habit and got shipped off to jail or prison with other people who were in the same toxic cycle. In America, "prisons and jails are the largest institutions housing adults with serious mental health and/ or substance use disorders."[1]

OFTEN THE MOST TOXIC PEOPLE ARE PEOPLE WITH UNTREATED SOUL-WOUNDS.

I now have compassion for my dad. But at fourteen, I had contempt for him. I could not understand how he did not want to be in my life.

He was not there when I played in the 1996 AFC Championship game, one game from playing in the Super Bowl.

He was not there when I played in the biggest game in BYU football history in 1990 when we defeated the top-ranked Miami Hurricanes.

He was not there when I played in the 1988 Texas high school football state championship game.

In fact, one of my fondest memories of playing football is when in fifth grade my dad came to see me play in the flag football championship. On the last play of the game, I scored the winning touchdown. My teammates carried me off the field. That was the last football game my dad ever saw me play.

In eighth grade, he showed up to one of my middle school basketball games. He sat next to Mom. I did not play well, and after the game, he came into the locker room and talked to my coach. As

---

[1] Tanya St. John, "Why America's Largest Mental Health Institutions Are Prisons and Jails," August 8, 2016, https://www.arundellodge.org /why-americas-largest-mental-health-institutions-are-prisons-and-jails /#:~:text=In%20the%20U.S.%2C%20prisons%20and,America's%20 prison%20and%20jail%20beds (accessed December 2, 2020).

he talked to my coach, he leaned up against the wall with left arm extended bracing himself. His long sleeve shirt rolled down his arm, revealing his heroin tracks. My coach and I made eye contact, both pretending to not see what we saw. I decided in that locker room, on that day, that I did not need him.

I was lying to myself.

But then again, we lie to ourselves when the truth is too painful to bear.

Unresolved pain breaks our resolve.

Find Your Father

In the early 2000s, I was sitting at my desk writing letters to my family and friends about my newfound love relationship with Jesus. I wanted everyone to know that Jesus forgives, that Jesus lives, that Jesus loves. During this euphoric moment, I heard a voice that said, "Find your father." I stood up and started cursing in an empty room, saying things like,

"Why should I find my father?"

"Where was he when I needed a dad?"

"Where was he when I needed someone to teach me how to be a man?"

Before I knew it, I found myself balled up on the floor with tears streaming down my face. In that moment of brokenness, vulnerability, and honesty, I sensed Abba saying,

"You are right. Your father does not deserve you looking to find him or your forgiveness. But Dewey, never forget, *you did not deserve my Son finding and forgiving you*. Now, get up, son. Go find your daddy."

I knew that finding and forgiving my father was the right thing to do, but I did not want to.

I wanted to stay angry.

I wanted to keep holding onto my grudge.

I wanted to keep withholding forgiveness because it gave me a sense of power and control.

But it was all a lie. I had no power or control. I was being controlled by the power of unforgiveness. Any power that is unforgiving is not the power of Abba. It is from the father of lies, the evil one. I did not feel like forgiving my father, but I knew it was the right thing to do. God wanted me to be free. And I wanted to be free.

**ANY POWER THAT IS UNFORGIVING
IS NOT THE POWER OF ABBA.
IT IS FROM THE FATHER OF
LIES, THE EVIL ONE.**

Carrying unforgiveness is like trying to swim with a five-hundred-pound anchor strapped to your back. I was sinking. It was time to rise.

Time to Forgive

My search for my father led me to a prison in Texas. I wrote him a short letter that essentially said, "Dad, I want you to know that I forgive you. I love you, and I want you to be a part of my life and to know your grandchildren." After a few weeks of no response from him, I figured he got the letter and threw it away. But one day, when I checked the mail, I saw a letter from him. I ran into the house, threw the other pieces of mail down, and went into my office. I began to read his letter, wiping away tears. Finally, I could see the words I had hoped to hear from him my whole life. He said, "Son, thank you for forgiving me. I do love you, and I do want to know my grandchildren." I cried and cried, letting go of decades of unforgiveness. The dam broke and rivers of peace flooded over me. Each tear was like a chain breaking, setting me free. When I cried and had no more tears to cry, I felt lighter. The burden of unforgiveness had been lifted.

We were not designed to hold on to unforgiveness. Unforgiveness is an infection that makes us soul-sick. Unforgiveness is an unwelcomed guest that stays too long and takes too much.

When we choose to forgive, we are unloading a burden we were never meant to carry. Friend, don't hold onto that burden any longer. Let Jesus carry it.

> And be kind and compassionate to one another, forgiving one another, just as God also forgave you in Christ. (Eph. 4:32)

My father and I made up for lost time. Our relationship was restored. He did the best he could. I had never known his pain or his struggle. We loved each other. Before he died, he played a game of Checkers with the grandkids at a restaurant. I will always remember the smiles on my kids' faces and the peace that was on his, and the healing that was in my heart.

Who do you need to forgive? How long will you carry the burden of unforgiveness? Today is the day that you can choose freedom by choosing to forgive.

Write that letter.

Make that call.

Go see that person.

Forgiveness *Is* a Process of Discovery

You cannot give away what you do not possess. Asking someone to forgive without the divine presence of Jesus present in them is like asking a man to jump to the moon.

> The one who has the Son has life. The one who does not have the Son of God does not have life. (1 John 5:12)

Divine forgiveness has its origin in Abba himself, revealed in the bloody cross and empty tomb of Jesus. You cannot muster up the strength to have this kind of forgiveness. This kind of forgiveness is not from willpower but from the power of the One who walked up a hill called Calvary. Abba's forgiveness in Messiah Jesus, by the Spirit's power, is a sheer gift. I was able to forgive my father because my Abba forgave me.

ABBA'S FORGIVENESS IN MESSIAH JESUS, BY THE SPIRIT'S POWER, IS A SHEER GIFT.

> Make allowance for each other's faults, and forgive anyone who offends you. Remember, the Lord forgave you, so you must forgive others. (Col. 3:13 NLT)

Oh, to be forgiven by Jesus is the sweetest of the sweet. To be cleansed under the flood of his blood.

> Oh, what joy for those whose disobedience is forgiven, whose sin is put out of sight! (Ps. 32:1 NLT)

In forgiveness, we experience the uniqueness of Abba and his grace. Grace is Abba opening our spiritual eyes "to understand, as all God's people should, how wide, how long, how high, and how deep his love is" (Eph. 3:18 NLT). Marinate on the Spirit-inspired words of the prophet Micah that guide us into the heart of Abba and how he forgives us.

> Where is another God like you,
>> who pardons the guilt of the remnant,
>> overlooking the sins of his special people?
> You will not stay angry with your people forever,
>> because you delight in showing unfailing
>> love.
> Once again you will have compassion on us.
>> You will trample our sins under your feet
>> and throw them into the depths of the
>> ocean!
> You will show us your faithfulness and unfailing
>> love
> as you promised to our ancestors Abraham and
>> Jacob long ago.
> (Mic. 7:18–20 NLT)

We Discover We Are Pardoned in Christ Jesus

Have you noticed that when an American president prepares to leave office, he will give pardons? The President of the United States, under the Constitution, has the power to set aside the punishment for federal crimes. Abba in Christ Jesus has pardoned you and me from our cosmic treason against him.

Sin is not a small thing. It is treason of the highest order. That is why the Most High himself ordered the sacrifice of Jesus. In the love-fueled sacrifice of Jesus, Abba granted us an eternal pardon (Mic. 7:18).

> For he has rescued us from the kingdom of darkness and transferred us into the Kingdom of his dear Son, who purchased our freedom and forgave our sins. (Col. 1:13–14 NLT)

We have been *rescued* from darkness.
We have been *transferred* into the Kingdom of Jesus.
We have been *purchased* and set free from sin and death.
We have been *forgiven* so we can forgive.

When we pray, "And forgive us our debts [sins]," we are entering the inner sanctum of Abba's heart to forgive us, to restore us, to love us.

> He has not dealt with us as our sins deserve or repaid us according to our iniquities. For as high as the heavens are above the earth, so great is his faithful love toward those who fear him. As far as the east is from the west, so far has he removed our transgressions from us. (Ps. 103:10–12)

We Discover That We Are at Peace with Abba in Christ Jesus

One of the hardest things I ever had to do as a parent is discipline my kids. They both have beautiful brown eyes, and they would give me that look that would just melt my heart. But I knew that a good father disciplines his children because he loves them. I could not, and cannot, stay angry with them. They are my heart. Before they even ask, I have forgiven them. Likewise, but in a way that is a trillion times purer and more beautiful, Abba has an eternally kind disposition toward us. He is not angry with those of us in Christ. We have peace with Abba because King Jesus was our peace offering (Mic. 7:18).

> Therefore, since we have been made right in God's sight by faith, we have peace with God because of what Jesus Christ our Lord has done for us. (Rom. 5:1 NLT)

ABBA HAS AN ETERNALLY KIND DISPOSITION TOWARD US. HE IS NOT ANGRY WITH THOSE OF US IN CHRIST. WE HAVE PEACE WITH ABBA BECAUSE KING JESUS WAS OUR PEACE OFFERING.

We Discover That Abba Delights in Showing Unfailing Love to Those in Christ

My grandmother, Ossie B. Gilliam, and I were so close that I called her just about every day from the day I left for college until she died. She loved it when I would come home to see her. Sometimes during our phone calls, the doorbell would ring, and she would tell me to hold on as she went to see who was at the door. When she got to the door, it was me! She would light up and say, "Dewey, I am gonna whoop you for surprising me!" I delighted in surprising my grandmother.

Abba delights in showing us his unfailing love (Mic. 7:18). How will you know? You will experience the love of Christ in such a way that all other loves fail to compare (Phil. 3:7–8). In God's kingdom, forgiveness is spelled LOVE.

We Discover the Epic Compassion That Abba Has for Those in Christ Jesus

The prophet Micah tells us Abba will have "compassion on us" and "trample our sins" (Mic. 7:19). The Hebrew word for compassion, *racham*, paints a picture that describes the pity a parent has for a child. It is as if Abba looks at our self-engineered sinful mess and his heart toward us is one of love, pity, and grace. Abba has compassion on us, even though we do not deserve it. Abba is a warrior who destroys our sins.

 ABBA HAS COMPASSION ON US, EVEN THOUGH WE DO NOT DESERVE IT.

When we pray "forgive us our debts," we are praying to our Creator God, who is compassionate, merciful, gracious, and active in forgiving and restoring us.

> Be gracious to me, God,
> according to your faithful love;
> according to your abundant compassion,
> blot out my rebellion.
> Completely wash away my guilt
> and cleanse me from my sin. (Ps. 51:1–2)

We Discover That Abba Has Thrown Our Sins into the Sea

I love finding ponds, especially out in the country. Those country ponds have the best fishing. One of the worst disappointments is finding one that I know is loaded with largemouth bass and seeing a sign that says, "No Fishing." Similarly, Abba does not want you fishing for the sins he has thrown into the depths of the sea of his forgotten memory. In the flood of Jesus' blood, your sins were washed away and thrown "into the depths of the ocean!" (Mic. 7:19 NLT). So please stop reminding yourself of your past sins. King Jesus has placed a "No Fishing" sign over your sins. Forget what he has forgotten. You are forgiven.

ABBA DOES NOT WANT YOU FISHING FOR THE SINS HE HAS THROWN INTO THE DEPTHS OF THE SEA OF HIS FORGOTTEN MEMORY.

> I will never again remember their sins and their lawless acts. (Heb. 10:17)

We Discover That Abba Keeps His Covenant with Those in Christ

Has someone ever made you a promise and broken it? People make and break promises all the time. Like you, I have broken promises, too. But you will never have to worry about Abba breaking his promises. He is the only true promise-keeper. He is the covenant-maker and the covenant-keeper.

The prophet Micah writes that Abba will show his "unfailing love as [he] promised to our ancestors Abraham and Jacob long ago" (Mic. 7:20 NLT). In Genesis 11, Abba's family is lost as they built a city to create a kingdom apart from him. In Genesis 12:1–3, Abba promises Abraham that through him, he is getting his family back. This new family will be a colorful, multiethnic family that will become the body of Christ, the Church.

Yahweh is unrelenting in keeping his covenant.

Abba's covenantal love is unfailing, loyal, and true.

He will never forsake us.

He made a promise that is unbreakable because he holds us in his nail-pierced hands.

He will not fail to reconcile all those who trust in Jesus (Rom. 10:13). Anyone and everyone are welcome to participate in this New Covenant family (Gal. 3:8, 26–29). When Jesus' blood is shed on the cross, he not only forgives our sins, but he also recreates us and places us in his new family. On the night Jesus was betrayed, he said, "This cup is the new covenant in my blood, which is poured out for you" (Luke 22:20).

Jesus is the "guarantee of a better covenant" (Heb. 7:22).

When we pray "forgive us of our debts," we are experiencing more than forgiveness. We are entering into Abba's world, on Abba's terms, for Abba's glory. In living in, for, and from Abba's glory, we truly begin to live.

> A thief comes only to steal and kill and destroy. I
> have come so that they may have life and have it
> in abundance. (John 10:10)

We Discover That Jesus Is the Fulfillment to All of Abba's Promises

Seemingly out of nowhere the term "fake news" became a normative phrase in the American vocabulary. Just as there is "fake news," let's understand that there are fake gospels.

> But even if we or an angel from heaven should preach to you a gospel contrary to what we have preached to you, a curse be on him! (Gal. 1:8)

The most common and pernicious fake gospel is the *Prosperity Gospel*. The Prosperity Gospel tells you that God wants you wealthy and healthy. All you must do is have enough faith. But if you do not have enough faith, you will not receive the wealth and health that is yours. The Prosperity Gospel does not talk about sin in the biblical sense, and the salvation it offers doesn't hold a candle to the true salvation we have in Christ.

There is another fake gospel that I call *The Life Coach Jesus Gospel*. Life Coach Jesus makes sure that upper-middle-class people fulfill their dreams and raise good families. Jesus is more of a self-help motivational guy than a redeeming savior or king. He simply hangs around to help you get the American dream. Life Coach Jesus is good at giving you pithy statements that become Instagram memes on how to live your best life. Again, this is "fake news," not Good News.

Finally, there is the fake gospel that I call *American Political Jesus Gospel*. American Political Jesus can come in the guise of a left-leaning progressive or right-leaning conservative. The progressives want God's kingdom without a bloody cross and supernatural resurrection, and conservatives want to save souls without remembering that Jesus saves the whole person. The left wants justice without Jesus. The right wants moral order without grace. American Political Jesus is all about who is in the White House or Supreme Court. Politics is the new religion of America. This is "fake news," not Good News.

The Good News is that Abba made a promise to pursue and purchase a family for himself through a pagan named Abraham. Abraham and his family worshiped false gods (Josh. 24:2), but at Abba's invitation of grace, he entered into a covenant with the One True God.

THE GOOD NEWS IS THAT ABBA MADE A PROMISE TO PURSUE AND PURCHASE A FAMILY FOR HIMSELF THROUGH A PAGAN NAMED ABRAHAM.

> As it is written: I have made you the father of
> many nations. (Rom. 4:17)

Through the family line of Abraham, Israel was born with a mission. That mission was to be a kingdom of priests reflecting God's glory to those lost in darkness (Exod. 19:4–6). Instead of being the light to those in darkness, however, Israel often found itself lost in the darkness of idolatry.

But Abba is unrelenting in the pursuit of his family from many different people groups because he is the God of covenant-making and covenant-keeping. Israel failed in her mission, continually falling away from God. So, Abba sent his Son on a new mission to be the light of the world (John 8:12) and to redeem his family.

In King Jesus, Abba's covenant is kept. All who trust in Jesus become children of Abraham, regenerated, redeemed, and righteous. Abraham's children are a forgiven, New Covenant family. Jesus, with his bloody cross and empty tomb, is the fulfillment of Abba's promise. What was lost in the garden will be restored as an epic city, and God will dwell with his people (Rev. 21:1–4).

> For every one of God's promises is "Yes" in him. Therefore, through him we also say "Amen" to the glory of God. Now it is God who strengthens us together with you in Christ, and who has anointed us. He has also put his seal on us and given us the Spirit in our hearts as a down payment. (2 Cor. 1:20–22)

In Messiah Jesus, we have been forgiven. Our lives are so woven into the life of Jesus that forgiveness is our new name.

In the next chapter, we are going to discover what forgiveness is not, and how we, as Abba's kids, can live as faithful witnesses in a world that needs the forgiveness we possess.

─────────────── Marinate on This ───────────────

Prayer

Abba,

Your sacred Scriptures say,

Blessed are those whose lawless acts are forgiven and
whose sins are covered. Blessed is the person the
Lord will never charge with sin (Rom. 4:7–8).

Give me a heart that shows my appreciation of being forgiven by
being joyful and by being forgiving to those who have hurt me.

King Jesus,

I feel that my words are inadequate to express my love for you.
You purchased my freedom and forgiveness with your blood.
You became the sacrificial lamb that wiped away my sin.

Holy Spirit,

You are the down payment of my inheritance
in the new heavens and new earth.

You are the source of my strength to receive
forgiveness and to give forgiveness.

May I live in the power and beauty of forgiveness.

The next day John saw Jesus coming toward him
and said, "Look, the Lamb of God, who takes
away the sin of the world" (John 1:29).

In Jesus' name, amen.

Questions for Reflection

1. When was a time you found it extremely hard to forgive somebody? Why was that so challenging?

2. How does the forgiveness of God in Christ affect our ability to forgive others?

3. In relation to forgiveness, is the message of Christianity similar to or different than the world's message? In what ways?

4. Pastor Derwin used the analogy of going fishing in the sea of your forgiven sins. Have you ever been tempted to do this? Why is it important not to do this?

Things to Remember

1. Often the most toxic people are people with untreated soul-wounds.

2. Abba's forgiveness in Messiah Jesus, by the Spirit's power, is a sheer gift.

3. Abba has an eternally kind disposition toward us. He is not angry with those of us in Christ. We have peace with Abba because King Jesus was our peace offering.

4. In King Jesus, Abba's covenant is kept. All who trust in Jesus become children of Abraham, regenerated, redeemed, and righteous. Abraham's children are a forgiven, New Covenant

family. Jesus, with his bloody cross and empty tomb, is the fulfillment of Abba's promise. What was lost in the garden will be restored as an epic city, and God will dwell with his people.

CHAPTER 14

Forgiveness Matters

 In the last chapter, I told about my relationship with my father. I knew I needed to forgive him, but I did not want to even though I knew that being a follower of Jesus meant that I should.

Have you ever felt like me? I have learned that the pain of living with unforgiveness takes a physical and spiritual toll. Medical studies have found that living in a state of unforgiveness increases the risk of heart attack, messes up our cholesterol levels, disrupts our sleep, increases pain in our bodies, raises our blood pressure, and increases our levels of anxiety, depression, and stress.[1]

LIVING WITH UNFORGIVENESS TAKES A PHYSICAL AND SPIRITUAL TOLL.

Literally, unforgiveness kills us—and the devil loves it.

Jesus knows that forgiveness, generated from his resurrection life, is good for us. But it's still really hard! And how do we do it?

---

[1] John Hopkins Medicine, "Forgiveness: Your Health Depends on It," https://www.hopkinsmedicine.org/health/wellness-and-prevention/forgiveness-your-health-depends-on-it (accessed December 14, 2020).

Remember People Are Broken Just Like You

Have you ever wondered why children have to be taught virtues such as kindness, sharing, selflessness? The reason is that we are broken in need of divine repair. The reason why people hurt each other is because, at our core, we are corrupted, devoid of the life of God himself. Jesus did not simply come to make bad people good. Jesus came to make dead people alive (Eph. 2:1–6).

Even in a broken world, filled with broken people, and forces of evil, we are going to collide in ways that require us to forgive each other.

Remember Forgiven People Forgive People

My capacity to forgive people who have hurt me is only as great as my memory of how much Jesus has forgiven me. When I try to get on my high horse, the Holy Spirit reminds me of who I used to be, the things I did to cause pain, bringing me back down to earth.

> Make allowance for each other's faults, and forgive anyone who offends you. Remember, the Lord forgave you, so you must forgive others. (Col. 3:13 NLT)

Discover the Humanity of the Offender

One step that can help us to learn to practice forgiveness is to remember that those who mistreat others are themselves often the products of mistreatment.

What happened to the person who hurt you? Unhealed hurts make hurters.

It is a grand and beautiful thing when God the Holy Spirit helps us to look at our offenders the way Jesus looked at us when we offended him. With an eternal gaze of grace, Abba looks upon us with eyes of compassion. A great pity wells up in his heart. He sees how we're responding out of the un-dealt-with damage from sins committed against us. This leads us to act out against others.

Jesus comes to undo the damage.

But before he does, on the cross, all the damage you have inflicted on others and that has been poured out on you is placed on him.

The cross of Jesus is the place where *all* sin was dealt with once and for all.

What Forgiveness Is Not

Maybe you have experienced an unspeakable wound at the hands of another. I am sorry. I hurt for you.

Abba knows that forgiving what seems unforgivable is hard, and this is why God the Holy Spirit indwells you. He is the living presence and power of Abba to enable you to do what you can never do on your own (Heb. 9:14; 1 Cor. 3:16–17). God's grace is sufficient to forgive your sins and give you the power to forgive those who have sinned against you. Also, he is the power that moves you to ask for forgiveness when you hurt another.

GOD'S GRACE IS SUFFICIENT TO FORGIVE YOUR SINS AND GIVE YOU THE POWER TO FORGIVE THOSE WHO HAVE SINNED AGAINST YOU.

From the pages of my own life and nearly two decades of pastoral counseling, I have found that there are misunderstandings about what forgiveness is. Let us clear up some of these untruths.

Forgiveness is not an emotion or a feeling.
Forgiveness is a commitment to Abba's glory.

Forgiveness is not an emotion or a feeling. Forgiveness is a Holy-Spirit-enabled commitment to Abba's glory because he has forgiven us in Messiah Jesus. When we choose to forgive, we are choosing to glorify our Abba. There will be times that we do not feel like forgiving the person who hurt us. In fact, *feelings* of forgiveness may not follow the action of forgiveness for a long, long time. But our commitment to forgive is not found in our feelings; it is found in the forgiveness that God spilled his blood for (Matt. 6:14).

Forgiven people forgive people.

Forgiveness is not faking like you were not wounded. Forgiveness is being honest about your pain.

Forgiveness is not faking like the person who wounded you did not hurt you. Often, when someone apologizes to us, we're tempted to say things like "it's okay," "don't worry about it," or "no big deal." But notice—all of these responses are a way of minimizing the offense, shrugging off the sin. None of them are true forgiveness, which requires an honest acknowledgment of the pain caused.

God didn't respond to our sin by shrugging it off with a "no worries." No, his forgiveness of us cost him dearly, because of the greatness of the offense. Forgiveness requires being honest about the pain caused.

For a long time, I pretended my dad's absence did not hurt me. When I finally got honest about my pain, Jesus began to do soul surgery on me. He moved me from anger toward my father to compassion for my father. Ignoring pain does not make it go away. Asking Abba to help us by his Spirit and working with trusted counselors can help us walk through the pain toward healing.

Forgiveness is not excusing what the person did to you or allowing them to keep hurting you.

When you forgive the person who injured you, you are not excusing what they did to you. When you forgive, you are refusing to allow them to re-injure you by holding on to the hurt. When you forgive, you are saying the pain of the past stops today. I will not carry this pain around anymore.

Years ago, I was counseling a person who was sexually molested by her father. I do not have the categories to even imagine the hell this person experienced. This person had lived with the wounds of sexual abuse for six decades. She would describe how she wanted to burn her father alive so he could experience the same hell she did. This bitter root of unforgiveness was like a ghost that haunted her.

Vengeance does not bring the healing you need.

Revenge turns you into the person that you hate.

Bitterness is like drinking nuclear waste and hoping that the person you are mad at gets radiation poisoning. Bitterness only kills the bitter person. Forgiveness is you saying, "I will not allow you to hurt me all over again by replaying the pain you caused me. I am giving you to Abba. You will not rent space in my mind anymore; it is too expensive. You have cost me too much. Christ lives in me. You are not welcome here anymore."

Forgiveness is not entrusting yourself to the person who hurt you. Forgiveness creates boundaries.

Forgiveness does not mean that you put your heart in a place to be trampled on again by the person who wounded you. Forgiveness is given as a gift of grace. Trust is earned over time through repentance and transformation.

I have seen abusers misuse the gift of forgiveness. For years, a wife verbally and physically abused her husband. (I have also seen the roles reversed. Abuse, both verbally and physically, is always wrong. The church should be a community of healing and help.) The husband was abused by his mother, so he normalized verbal and physical abuse. The cycle of abuse went like this: the wife gets angry and punches him in the face. Then she apologizes. He requests to see a counselor, but she refuses to get help. The cycle repeats itself, over and over.

As children came along, they were witnesses to this toxic environment. Eventually, the husband grew in his identity in Christ and woke up to the reality that he should not be a human punching bag or an object of verbal abuse. Abusers—male and female—can not only hurt you physically, but they can also attack your self-worth making you feel like you deserve to be treated violently and disrespectfully. Through therapy and pastoral counseling, he learned to develop emotional boundaries to protect his heart and his children. When he developed boundaries, his wife finally sought help.

Thankfully in this situation, there was a restoration of trust and relationship—but that is not always the case. Forgiveness does not mean allowing yourself to remain in a situation where you are physically, verbally, or emotionally abused.

FORGIVENESS DOES NOT MEAN ALLOWING YOURSELF TO REMAIN IN A SITUATION WHERE YOU ARE PHYSICALLY, VERBALLY, OR EMOTIONALLY ABUSED.

Forgiveness is not alleviating the person from the consequences of harming you. It is entrusting the person to Abba.

The person who hurt you is responsible for the harm they caused. Let God be the judge and jury. He is much more just than you could ever be. Leave them in the merciful hands of Abba. When a person sins and hurts you, they are first and foremost sinning against God.[2]

Forgive them and give them to God. Dark powers want you to get even with the person who hurt you, but hurt for hurt only multiplies pain. The cycle of hurt ends when we choose forgiveness.

---

[2] It is important to clarify something here: God is the ultimate Judge and Jury, but he also exercises his authority through earthly authorities that have a mandate to execute justice. By God's grace, though our governing authorities are imperfect, they do exist to protect people from harm. While you should leave it up to God to judge people who sin against you, there are some sins that also have legal consequences now—specifically, sins that are crimes. In those cases—including when anyone is physically harming you in any way—you ought to notify the proper earthly authorities to bring justice against the crime committed and prevent future harm. Likewise, if you are ever in a position where you learn that someone is committing a crime against someone else, you should notify the authorities.

DARK POWERS WANT YOU TO GET EVEN WITH THE PERSON WHO HURT YOU, BUT HURT FOR HURT ONLY MULTIPLIES PAIN. THE CYCLE OF HURT ENDS WHEN WE CHOOSE FORGIVENESS.

> Friends, do not avenge yourselves; instead, leave room for God's wrath, because it is written, Vengeance belongs to me; I will repay, says the Lord. But "If your enemy is hungry, feed him. If he is thirsty, give him something to drink. For in so doing you will be heaping fiery coals on his head." (Rom. 12:19–20)

Forgiving the Unforgivable

In 1994, the country of Rwanda became the scene of a horrific act of evil. The ethnic Hutus killed as many as 800,000 people of the mostly Tutsi minority. Rivers ran red with blood.

In this evil, a Rwandan pastor returned home to his war-torn nation to bring about peace and reconciliation through the gospel of Jesus Christ.[3] Because he was an ethnic Hutu teaching peace and reconciliation, many of his kinsmen thought he was working undercover for the Tutsis.[4] He was viewed as a traitor to the Hutus. He was tortured three times by his own people. Despite the persecution and violence, he continued to preach the gospel of peace and

---

[3] Jeff Hartman, "Meet the Leader," http://www.worldnextdoor.org/magazine/june-2013/ignite/celestins-story/ (accessed December 12, 2020).

[4] Hartman, "Meet the Leader."

reconciliation. He believed that only the cross of Jesus was strong enough to turn enemies into friends and foes into family (Eph. 2:14–17).

But his trust in Jesus, his gospel, and his kingdom were put to the test in 1997 when five members of his family and seventy members of his church were murdered in revenge killings.[5]

Could he practice what he preached?

Was the gospel strong enough to work in his life?

He knew he had to forgive them—and he did.

But about a year later, while teaching in a seminary about peace and reconciliation through Jesus, he came face-to-face with some of the men who killed his family.[6] They were in his seminary learning. By God's grace, he forgave them. He also freed himself from anger, bitterness, and revenge.

> Do not be conquered by evil, but conquer evil with good. (Rom. 12:21)

Evil is not overcome by evil.

Evil is overcome by love.

Love always wins, even when it seems like it loses.

How do I know? Because the Nazarene died on a cross for the sins of the world, but he walked out of a tomb to give the world his resurrection life.

---

[5] Hartman, "Meet the Leader."
[6] Hartman, "Meet the Leader."

Freedom and Forgiveness

Freedom

As Americans, when we think of freedom, we often think it means the unhindered ability to do what we want to do. This is what's called "negative freedom"—freedom *from* something. However, the true freedom that Abba grants us in his kingdom is the freedom to worship him. It is "positive freedom"—freedom *to*. In Christ, we are free *to* worship Abba, and we all become like what we worship.

The story of God is a story of freedom, but it comes at a great cost.

When the children of Israel were slaves in Egypt under the oppression of Pharaoh, not only were they being mistreated, but Abba's covenant promise to give Abraham a family was being threatened. The children of Israel were the key to setting the world free from serving dead idols. Through Moses, Abba sent ten plagues against Egypt, triumphing over the Egyptian gods (Exod. 6:6–8). Despite Pharaoh's arrogance and evil, Abba was merciful to Pharaoh.

The God of Abraham, the covenant-maker and covenant-keeper, honored his word and relented from the plagues. But when Pharaoh saw Abba's mercy, he abused it and did not honor his word. It was Abba's mercy that hardened Pharaoh's heart. The more we abuse God's mercy, the harder our hearts get. Pharoah did not heed Abba's warning. He took advantage of God's mercy and the more he did, the harder his heart grew. God "hardened his heart similar to the way the sun hardens clay and also melts wax. If Pharaoh had been receptive to God's warnings, his heart would not have been hardened by God. But when God gave Pharaoh a reprieve from the plagues, he took advantage of the situation."[7]

> But when Pharaoh saw there was relief, he hardened his heart and would not listen to them, as the LORD had said. (Exod. 8:15)

The final Egyptian god to be defeated was Pharaoh himself. Pharaohs believed they were gods. Therefore, their sons were gods.

> I told you: "Let my son go so that he may worship me, but you refused to let him go. Look, I am about to kill your firstborn son!" (Exod. 4:23)

Before this plague comes, Abba instructs his people to select an unblemished sheep or goat to slaughter and to put its blood "on the two doorposts" of their homes (Exod. 12:5, 7).

> "I will pass through the land of Egypt on that night and strike every firstborn male in the land of Egypt, both people and animals. I am the LORD; I will execute judgments against all the gods of Egypt. The blood on the houses where you are staying will be a distinguishing mark for you; when I see the blood, I will pass over you. No plague will be among you to destroy you when I strike the land of Egypt." (Exod. 12:12–13)

After the final false Egyptian god was defeated with the death of all the first-born in Egypt, including Pharaoh's own son, Pharaoh

---

[7] Norman L. Geisler, "Pharaoh, Hardening of," in *Baker Encyclopedia of Christian Apologetics* (Grand Rapids, MI: Baker Books, 1999), 592.

finally lets Abba's family go so they can worship him and continue their mission.

It was the blood that set Abba's kids free.

This act is called the Passover, and it is the most celebrated event in the history of Israel (Exod. 12:12–20). Passover is when Abba frees his people *from* slavery *for* worship. The apostle Paul draws the connection to Christ when he calls Christ "our Passover lamb" (1 Cor. 5:7). In the New Covenant, Jesus, the true and better Lamb of God, sheds his own blood to free us *from* something bigger and worse than pharaoh, and to free us *to* worship him in spirit and in truth. King Jesus frees us from sin, death, and the evil one.

You are no longer under the evil slave master.

You are now free under King Jesus.

The blood of the unblemished Lamb sets you free to worship and to become like the one you worship. Peter writes,

> For you know that you were redeemed from your empty way of life inherited from your ancestors, not with perishable things like silver or gold, but with the precious blood of Christ, like that of an unblemished and spotless lamb. . . . Since you have purified yourselves by your obedience to the truth, so that you show sincere brotherly love for each other, from a pure heart love one another constantly, because you have been born again—not of perishable seed but of imperishable—through the living and enduring word of God. (1 Pet. 1:18–23)

THE BLOOD OF THE UNBLEMISHED LAMB SETS YOU FREE TO WORSHIP AND TO BECOME LIKE THE ONE YOU WORSHIP.

Forgiveness

Do you have Jewish friends who celebrate the Day of Atonement, or Yom Kippur? On this holy day, in ancient Israel, the high priest would enter the Holy of Holies in the temple, where the presence of God dwelt, and place the blood of sacrificed animals on the cover of the ark, called the mercy seat. For the Jewish people, the tabernacle, and later the temple, was where heaven and earth met. It was the place of worship, forgiveness, cleansing, purification, communal identification, and transformation.

It was the place where the blood of the lamb forgave sins and cleaned sinners.

It was a place of grace.

> Atonement will be made for you on this day to cleanse you, and you will be clean from all your sins before the Lord. (Lev. 16:30)

The temple was a place that pointed to the greater Lamb that would be sacrificed for the sins of the world. When John the Baptist saw Jesus, he said, "Look, the Lamb of God, who takes away the sin of the world!" (John 1:29). The blood of Jesus, who brings us the New Covenant, cleanses you, purifies you, and declares you righteous (Rom. 5:9). This grace places us in the new people of Abba. We are a community of forgiveness. You are included in and participate in a family of atonement that knows that there is no forgiveness of sin "without the shedding of blood" (Heb. 9:22). There is purifying power in the blood of Jesus (Heb. 9:14).

He is the ultimate and final sacrificial lamb (Heb. 9:27–28).

He is the ultimate temple (Heb. 9:12).

He is the ultimate high priest (Heb. 9:11).

He is the ultimate mercy seat (Heb. 9:23–28).

He is the one and only Son whose blood transforms us into Abba's kids.

> [Jesus] entered the most holy place once for all time, not by the blood of goats and calves, but by his own blood, having obtained eternal redemption. . . . how much more will the blood of Christ, who through the eternal Spirit offered himself without blemish to God, cleanse our consciences from dead works so that we can serve the living God? (Heb. 9:12, 14)

When we pray, "Forgive us our debts, as we also have forgiven our debtors," we are affirming that we are included in Abba's family, the family that celebrates the eternal Passover and eternal Day of Atonement in Messiah Jesus.

The story of Jesus, the Lamb of God, is the story that provides our forgiveness.

It's the story that gives us the power to extend forgiveness to those who have hurt us.

Forgiveness is a way of being for those who are forgiven.

—————— Marinate on This ——————

Prayer

Abba,

Today and for all eternity

I stand in the flood of the Lamb's blood.

He purifies me

He cleanses me

He forgives me.

In him, forgiven is my name, and when
I forgive, I spread his fame.

The toxic cycle of violence and vengeance is only
broken by the power of the Lamb's blood.

Holy Spirit,

Give me the grace to forgive as I have been forgiven.

May I live as a person who walks in the eternal
Passover and Eternal Day of Atonement.

King Jesus,

You are the Lamb of God who takes away the sins of the world.

You are the Passover Lamb.

In you, I am forgiven to forgive.

Amen.

Questions for Reflection

1. What did you learn in this chapter that might help you to be more forgiving to others?

2. What is the difference in actually forgiving someone and feeling like forgiving them?

3. What is the relationship between our freedom and our forgiveness as Christians? What have we been freed *from* and what have we been freed *to*?

4. How is our forgiveness possible? What did God do to accomplish it?

Things to Remember

1. Living with unforgiveness takes a physical and spiritual toll.

2. God's grace is sufficient to forgive your sins and give you the power to forgive those who have sinned against you.

3. The blood of the unblemished Lamb sets you free to worship and to become like the one you worship.

4. When we pray, "Forgive us our debts, as we also have forgiven our debtors," we are affirming that we are included in Abba's family, the family that celebrates the eternal Passover and Eternal Day of Atonement in Messiah Jesus.

SECTION V

Developing a Wartime Mindset

*"And do not bring us into temptation,
but deliver us from the evil one."*
MATTHEW 6:13

As this section unfolds, we will discover that Jesus holds us in his vast strength. No temptation is too great because we will learn how to put on Christ and resist temptation (Rom. 13:14). We will discover the three temptations Satan uses to undermine our faith. Finally, we will put on our battle armor because we are in a war. God has given us special armor to wear so we can be effective in our already promised victory (Eph. 6:10–20).

CHAPTER 15

Developing a Wartime Mindset

My grandmother got me hooked on *Mutual of Omaha's Wild Kingdom*, one of the most epic animal and nature shows ever. Each week we would gather around our TV set and be teleported to exotic parts of the world to see wild animals in their natural habitats. This show taught me about lions and how they hunt. The male lions were the protectors of the pride, but primarily it was the smaller, faster lionesses that were the hunters. The lionesses, in a coordinated, strategic method, surrounded their prey, closed in, and killed them. Their goal was to isolate and separate the prey from the herd. For example, the lionesses knew that one wildebeest could not stand a chance against their schemes.

The devil works the same way. The devil cannot steal your salvation, but he can steal your happiness and effectiveness for Abba's kingdom. That's why the apostle Peter warned us about him, and compared him to a lion on the hunt:

> Be sober-minded, be alert. Your adversary the
> devil is prowling around like a roaring lion, look-
> ing for anyone he can devour. (1 Pet. 5:8)

Dark powers desire to isolate and separate us from the herd, our brothers and sisters in Christ. In Christ, we protect and strengthen each other.

> Resist him, firm in the faith, knowing that the same kind of sufferings are being experienced by your fellow believers throughout the world. The God of all grace, who called you to his eternal glory in Christ, will himself restore, establish, strengthen, and support you after you have suffered a little while. (1 Pet. 5:9–10)

Thankfully, Jesus restores, establishes, strengthens, and supports us.

DARK POWERS DESIRE TO ISOLATE AND SEPARATE US FROM THE HERD, OUR BROTHERS AND SISTERS IN CHRIST. IN CHRIST, WE PROTECT AND STRENGTHEN EACH OTHER.

What if one of the wildebeest said to the thousands of others, "Why are we running from a few lions when there are way more of us? What if instead of running from them, we stood close to each other in unity and started running full speed toward them? Our sheer numbers and powers will crush them. We will no longer be their prey!"

If only the wildebeest knew how powerful they were together, they would easily defeat the lionesses. Because of the wildebeest's ignorance, they become dinner.

Often, as followers of Jesus, because of our ignorance of how strong we are together in Christ, we become dinner for the forces of darkness. Instead of living out of our holiness in Christ Jesus, we are sabotaged by the enemy. Instead of living in the collective strength of the church, we decide to be lone rangers. Many of us have yet to realize and live in the power of Jesus, who defeated the dark powers and triumphs over the power of sin, and the power of his church, which protects us from the plans of the devil.

C. S. Lewis wrote,

> There are two equal and opposite errors into which our race can fall about the devils. One is to disbelieve in their existence. The other is to believe and to feel an excessive and unhealthy interest in them. They themselves are equally pleased by both errors and hail a materialist or a magician with the same delight.[1]

Spiritual warfare is real.

Be aware, but not afraid. Be cognizant, but don't become captivated.

Never forget, the cross was bloody, and the tomb is empty. Jesus won. We ride the coattails of his victory (Rom. 8:35–39).

The Three Temptations

There is an old saying, "If it ain't broke, don't fix it." I often think this is what the Accuser says to his demons who are assigned to destroy our witness. The dark powers strategically attack Abba's kids with three temptations. In *Emotionally Healthy Spirituality*, Pete Scazzero explains them as (1) I Am What I Do (Performance), (2) I Am What I Have (Possession), and (3) I Am What Others

---

[1] C. S. Lewis, *The Screwtape Letters* (originally 1942; this edition: New York: Harper Collins, 1996), ix.

Think (Popularity).[2] Apparently, the devil doesn't think he needs to update his strategy, because he's had so much success with this one.

One of the traps of the dark forces is to convince us that we are strong enough to fend off his assaults alone. The good news is that Jesus lived the life we could not and defeated the three temptations for us. By faith, Jesus reenacts his triumphant victory for us, in us and through us.

After Jesus was baptized in the Jordan River by John the Baptist, Abba said to him, "This is my beloved Son, with whom I am well-pleased" (Matt. 3:17). What a beautiful affirmation! Up to this point in Jesus' life, he had not started his public ministry. Yet, his Abba showered him with an affirmation of love. The key to overcoming the temptations of the dark powers is knowing that you are loved by Abba. When we forget the stunning love of Abba, we think something else will satisfy us more than him.

After Jesus was baptized, the Holy Spirit led him to the wilderness to be tempted by the devil (Matt. 4:1). As Israel, after the Passover event, went into the wilderness for forty years, Jesus was in the wilderness for forty days. Israel was tempted three times and three times the people disobeyed (Deut. 8:3; 6:16; 6:13). Jesus is tempted three times in the wilderness, but three times he obeys, demonstrating how he is the new, faithful Israel that obeys Abba in the wilderness. Jesus rewrites the story of Israel from one of disobedience, to one of obedience. Jesus overcomes the temptations of the dark one. By incorporation into his life and story, we are empowered by him to do the same.

---

[2] Pete Scazzero, *Emotionally Healthy Spirituality* (Nashville: Integrity Publishers, 2006), 75–77.

JESUS REWRITES THE STORY OF ISRAEL FROM ONE OF DISOBEDIENCE, TO ONE OF OBEDIENCE.

Temptation One: I Am What I Do (Performance)

After forty days of fasting, Jesus was hungry. The tempter said to him, "If you are the Son of God, tell these stones to become bread" (Matt. 4:3). The devil knew Jesus was hungry, and he wanted Jesus to use his own power to turn the stones into bread. *He wanted Jesus to base his life on his performance instead of Abba's provision.* We either live from Jesus' performance, or we die from our own.

Performance-based living is a life rooted in our own accomplishments.

A grace-based life is a life rooted in the accomplishments of Christ.

The beautiful obedience of Jesus stands in the place of our ugly disobedience.

Jesus defeated the first temptation by quoting the Old Testament: "It is written: Man must not live on bread alone but on every word that comes from the mouth of God" (Matt. 4:4). Jesus trusted his Abba's provision. He did not have to strive to make something happen. Jesus knew that his Abba deeply loved and treasured him. This fact is true of us, too. His grace is enough for us.

We are not what we do. We are what Christ has done for us.

Temptation Two: I Am What I Have (Possessions)

Greed is Satan's spawn. It says, "I am what I possess."

"Watch out and be on guard against all greed, because one's life is not in the abundance of his possessions." (Luke 12:15)

The tempter wants us to believe our lives are found in our possessions. However, Jesus wants us to know our lives are found in being possessed by him and in using our lives to serve others generously through our possessions.

In Jesus' period of testing, Satan took him to a high mountain and showed him all of the world and its splendor (Matt. 4:8–9). Jesus was a poor carpenter. The dark power was tempting Jesus with, "Are not tired of being poor? Are you not tired of the Jews being oppressed by the Romans? I can give you all this power! You can possess it all if you bow down and worship me." Jesus responds with, "Go away, Satan! For it is written: Worship the Lord your God, and serve only him" (Matt. 4:10). Jesus' allegiance was to his Abba.

Jesus won the war we could not. Three times Jesus resisted the devil by remembering Scripture and remembering that he is not what he does, he is not what others think, and he is not what he possesses. Because we are in Jesus, we are more than conquerors.

The Son of God was revealed for this purpose: to destroy the devil's works. (1 John 3:8)

When we pray, "do not bring us into temptation, but deliver us from the evil one" (Matt. 6:13), we are affirming Jesus' victory. In Christ, we are not helpless. He even gives us battle armor for the war.

Temptation Three: I Am What Others Think (Popularity)

I was discipling a young college athlete a few years ago. On the outside, you would think he was confident and self-assured. However, the reality was that he was racked with anxiety because he was addicted to what others thought about him. His thoughts were dominated by people's opinions of him. His self-esteem rocketed with a compliment and plummeted with criticism. His life hung on the words of people instead of on the Word of God.

This young man became a people-pleaser, and like most people-pleasers, he ended up angry with the people he tried to please because he either burnt himself out or would find himself doing things that he knew were not good for him. We experience the fresh breeze of freedom when Abba's view of us becomes the view with which we see ourselves. In Christ, our popularity does not matter, because Jesus is our identity.

IN CHRIST, OUR POPULARITY DOES NOT MATTER, BECAUSE JESUS IS OUR IDENTITY.

In temptation two, the devil took the Messiah "to the holy city, had him stand on the pinnacle of the temple, and said to him, 'If you are the Son of God, throw yourself down'" (Matt. 4:5–6). In essence, Satan tells Jesus, "Show everyone how big of a deal you are." Jesus responds with, "It is also written: Do not test the Lord your God" (Matt. 4:7).

Jesus was secure in his Abba's love, so the opinions of Satan or people did not sway him from accomplishing his Father's will. We are not what others say about us. We are what Christ has done for us and the love he speaks over us.

Battle Armor

I started hearing about Tom before I met him. People told me about this Puerto Rican guy from the Lower Eastside of Manhattan who had a servant's heart and loved people deeply. He served in just about every ministry at Transformation Church at different times.

I, along with our council of elder-pastors, saw a pastoral call on Tom's life. We ordained him as a pastor. A few years later he became our executive pastor. I call him the "Alignment to the Assignment Guy." He has the spiritual gifts of administration, leadership, and evangelism.

As we were ordaining Tom, something he said left a tattoo in my soul. He said, "Pastor, I will clean toilets here. The vision of loving God completely, ourselves correctly, and our neighbors compassionately has transformed my life and how I parent. My children are being transformed by the gospel of grace."

Tom has not always been Pastor Tom. In high school, he was a star basketball player. After an injury killed his dreams of being a college player, his self-esteem plummeted, and he descended into drug use to mask the pain. The drug use only sent him into a deeper state of hopelessness. No matter how high he got, it could not fill the hole in his heart.

Ultimately, Abba in his grace used Tom's mother to save his life. Tom was good at disguising his weight loss from the drug use by wearing three shirts at a time, but his mother knew he was not well. Every time she saw him, it crushed her. She could not stand to see him slowly killing himself. She told him, "Please, do not come to see me anymore. It is killing me to watch you kill yourself." Her sobering words woke Tom up to God's grace.

Tom started attending AA meetings. God used Tom's sponsor to lead him toward Jesus. He told him, "I will walk with you and never leave because that is the way God is." For 365 days, his sponsor walked with him helping him stay clean. This type of love opened Tom's heart to Jesus' rescuing love. Through the voices of other people who loved Jesus, Tom recognized that only the power of Jesus could save him from sin and fight off his demons. Tom has learned to cultivate a wartime mindset by daily putting on the armor of God. He has been sober for thirty-one years now through God's grace.

His Strength > Our Strength

In cultivating a wartime mindset, we must remember that because of Christ's vast power, we live in victory. Jesus does the fighting for us.

God is all-powerful. Satan is not.

God is present everywhere. Satan is not.

God is all-knowing. Satan is not.

God is sovereign. Satan is not.

God is greater than Satan. It is not even close.

> Finally, be strengthened by the Lord and by his vast strength. (Eph. 6:10)

The same Jesus that obliterated the works of the devil has graciously given you battle armor.

My senior year in high school, I did not go to the prom. When I tell people that story, they look at me with sad eyes and say, "How could you not go to the prom?" Growing up as a kid, I did not recall anyone in my family reminiscing about their prom night back in the day. I was one of the only males in my family to graduate high school. Besides, we couldn't afford a tux anyway. Going to prom requires that you dress for the occasion. Prom was an occasion I had no interest in because it was not valued in my immediate family.

Likewise, Abba has given his children a tux called the Armor of God, which prepares us for the occasion called spiritual warfare. God does not send us into this cosmic battle without the proper clothing. Spiritual warfare is real. Abba has given us the right clothing for the occasion. We just need to put it on.

> **SPIRITUAL WARFARE IS REAL.**
> **ABBA HAS GIVEN US THE RIGHT**
> **CLOTHING FOR THE OCCASION.**
> **WE JUST NEED TO PUT IT ON.**

Put on the full armor of God so that you can
stand against the schemes of the devil. (Eph. 6:11)

Every morning, with a sense of urgency, we are called to put on the armor of God. God's armor is better than Tony Stark's Iron Man armor because ours is real. It empowers us to stand against the schemes of the devil, which are the same old tired schemes: (1) I Am What I Do (Performance), (2) I Am What I Have (Possession), and (3) I Am What Others Think (Popularity). Each lie is countered by the truth of Scripture and our union with Messiah Jesus, our suit of armor. We do not need Iron Man; we have the God-man.

People Are Not the Enemy

In this spiritual battle that Jesus has already won, we must remember that people are not the enemy. Our war is against the cosmic powers of evil that *influence* and *use* people to sow seeds of darkness. Evil powers want us to fight people and see them as the enemy. Forces of darkness primarily target our minds. When our minds are influenced by these forces of darkness, we start treating people like the enemy.

People are pawns in Satan's hands when the power of the Holy Spirit and the indwelling life of Christ are not present (2 Cor. 4:4). However, even for believers, if one persists in sin, demons cannot possess you, but they can oppress you and influence you to keep dishonoring God. Repent quickly. Do not give the evil one any room in your life.

> **PEOPLE ARE NOT THE ENEMY. OUR WAR IS AGAINST THE COSMIC POWERS OF EVIL THAT INFLUENCE AND USE PEOPLE TO SOW SEEDS OF DARKNESS.**

The "schemes of the devil" involve a highly organized structure that is constantly waging war on believers. Satan's invisible army consists of vast numbers of spiritual beings in a hierarchy of rulers, powers, world rulers, and spirit forces.[3]

As children of Abba, because we are coheirs in Christ Jesus, we have been granted authority, power, and victory. We walk in faith, not fear of the darkness. As followers of Jesus, we are to join Jesus in freeing people from bondage, and it's impossible to free people you do not love (Matt. 5:44–45). Love compels us to fight *for* people, not *with* people. They are not the enemy.

---

[3] Ken Boa, *Conformed to His Image* (Grand Rapid: Zondervan Academic: 2020), 358.

> For our struggle is not against flesh and blood, but
> against the rulers, against the authorities, against
> the cosmic powers of this darkness, against evil,
> spiritual forces in the heavens. (Eph. 6:12)

Belt of Truth

Imagine you're in a battle. As you engage the enemy—trying to block their blows and swing your sword with all your might—your pants fall around your feet, tripping you. You would be killed in a moment! Every day, followers of Jesus are falling and being roughed up by dark forces, giving in to temptation because they are not wearing the belt of truth.

> For this reason take up the full armor of God, so
> that you may be able to resist in the evil day, and
> having prepared everything, to take your stand.
> Stand, therefore, with truth like a belt around
> your waist. (Eph. 6:13–14)

My friend Tom learned that the "scene of the crime" was his mind; therefore, he puts on the belt of truth daily. The battle begins in our minds, so we must make sure we are equipped with knowledge of God's truth first. According to the apostle Paul, the belt of truth is this: "In him you also were sealed with the promised Holy Spirit when you heard the word of truth, the gospel of your salvation, and when you believed" (Eph. 1:13). The belt of truth is the gospel, the good news that we are in Christ and sealed by the Holy Spirit. The assaults of the enemy cannot withstand our "in Christness," and the power of the Holy Spirit that indwells us. The same power that raised King Jesus from the dead is at work in us (Rom. 8:9–11)!

Breastplate of Righteousness

As I said above, the "scene of the crime" is your mind. In the cosmic battle, dark powers want to sabotage you by getting you to think of yourself outside of your "in Christness." Outside of Jesus, Tom's state was abysmal (Rom. 3:10). He was hopeless and far from God. So were we.

> But the blood of Jesus brought Tom and us near to the heart of Abba (Eph. 2:13).
>
> It also declared us as righteous as Jesus (Rom. 5:19).

The righteousness of Abba in Christ is a breastplate that protects our hearts from the enemy's assault of condemnation.

> Righteousness like armor on your chest. (Eph. 6:14)

Our "in Christness" transforms us into weapons of righteousness. The righteousness of Christ—that is, his faithfulness to the fulfill the law of God—is ours now (Rom. 3:22). The righteousness of Christ that we are incorporated into then becomes the life of righteousness that we begin to progressively live as we trust the Holy Spirit daily. A righteous life is a life of devotion to God, commitment to his kingdom, and justice toward your neighbor.

A RIGHTEOUS LIFE IS A LIFE OF DEVOTION TO GOD, COMMITMENT TO HIS KINGDOM, AND JUSTICE TOWARD YOUR NEIGHBOR.

And do not offer any parts of it to sin as weapons for unrighteousness. But as those who are alive from the dead, offer yourselves to God, and all the parts of yourselves to God as weapons for righteousness. (Rom. 6:13)

Gospel Shoes

Tom is passionate about people knowing and loving Jesus. When he met Jesus and had his life transformed, he could not help but want others to know him too. Abba's armor includes what I call gospel shoes.

And your feet sandaled with readiness for the gospel of peace. (Eph. 6:15)

When we share the gospel of peace, we are pushing back the darkness and freeing all those who trust the message of salvation. The gospel of peace is Abba reconciling us to himself and each other, across ethnic lines, class lines, and all other kinds of dividing lines. Satan cannot take your salvation, but he loves to create disunity between Abba's kids. Our defense in this battle is the blood.

The blood of Jesus is our peace (Eph. 2:14).

The blood of Jesus tears down the barriers that divide us (Eph. 2:14).

The blood of Jesus creates a new race of grace called the church (Eph. 2:15).

The blood of Jesus reconciles us to Abba and each other (Eph. 2:16).

The blood of Jesus transforms us into his family (Eph. 2:17–19).

The blood of Jesus transforms us into his new temple (Eph. 2:19–22).

God has given us gospel shoes to go and proclaim the gospel of peace.

Shield of Faith

One of the geniuses of Rome's military might was the large rectangular wooden shields that soldiers used in battle. The shields were four feet high, and the fronts were made of leather. The leather would "be wetted to quench any fiery darts launched against them."[4] When "Roman legionaries closed ranks, the front row holding shields forward and those behind them holding shields above them, they were virtually invulnerable to any attack from flaming arrows."[5]

When Paul says, "In every situation take up the shield of faith with which you can extinguish all the flaming arrows of the evil one" (Eph. 6:16), this imagery would have created a word picture of the shield of faith that protects you from the fiery weapons of the enemy. The shield of faith protects us from the assault of the enemy. He cannot make you sin. You can resist him in Abba's grace.

THE SHIELD OF FAITH PROTECTS US FROM THE ASSAULT OF THE ENEMY. HE CANNOT MAKE YOU SIN. YOU CAN RESIST HIM IN ABBA'S GRACE.

Tom has learned to put on the armor of God daily; so can you. It takes intentionality and discipline. Having the shield of faith does not mean you will not experience hardships—you will (John 16:33;

---

[4] C. S. Keener, *The IVP Bible Background Commentary: New Testament* (Downers Grove, IL: InterVarsity Press, 1993), Eph. 6:16.

[5] Keener, *The IVP Bible Background Commentary: New Testament.*

James 1:2–4; Rom. 5:3–5). However, Abba will give you the power to withstand them in his love.

Also, never forget that it is not about the size of your faith; it is about the size of the God your faith is in. Your faith is not primary. Jesus' faithfulness is. It is his faithfulness that we hitch our wagons to.

The Helmet of Salvation

I love playing football. Playing in the National Football League was a dream come true. As a football player, I had specialized equipment that was designed to protect me. I will never forget my helmet. One of my contemporaries, Buffalo Bills Hall of Fame running back Thurman Thomas lost his helmet at the start of Super Bowl XXVI. The Bills best player couldn't play because he didn't have his helmet! Later his helmet was found, thank goodness. What is my point? Every morning put on the helmet of salvation. Don't ever lose track of your helmet!

The helmet of salvation is the Spirit-enabled ability to protect your mind by being aware of and seeing yourself incorporated into the Messiah. You are positioned in him. All that is true of him is true of you, by grace through faith. Make sure to monitor your thought life by rejecting things like gossip, negative and condemning self-talk, and immoral thoughts. Instead marinate on "whatever is true, whatever is honorable, whatever is just, whatever is pure, whatever is lovely, whatever is commendable—if there is any moral excellence and if there is anything praiseworthy—dwell on these things" (Phil. 4:8).

Be confident in Abba.

Jesus is the victorious warrior. He defeated sin, death, and the evil one.

Take the helmet of salvation. (Eph. 6:17)

The Sword of the Spirit

My first mentor, Alan Bacon, gave me one of the greatest gifts I could ever receive. He gave me the gift of loving the Word of God. Every time we talked, he pointed me back to the Bible to feed my soul, to enlighten my mind, and to draw me deeper into the mystery of Abba's love.

How did Jesus defeat Satan in the wilderness? He quoted Scripture. The Word of God is the sword of the Spirit. The Word of God is an offensive weapon.

> And the sword of the Spirit—which is the word of God. (Eph. 6:17)

The sword of a Roman soldier was used to hurt and kill, whereas God's sword heals and gives life. However, against the dark powers, we are delivering death blows with the sword of the Spirit.

According to Jesus, the Bible is about him and his redeeming love.

> "You pore over the Scriptures because you think you have eternal life in them, and yet they testify about me. But you are not willing to come to me so that you may have life." (John 5:39–40)

Jesus is the center of Scripture. If we read Scripture and miss Jesus, we're misreading Scripture. If we point others to Scripture without pointing them to Jesus, we're misusing Scripture. The sword of the Spirit is a weapon against the world, the flesh, and the devil, and the only thing that can defeat these enemies of the cross of Christ.

The Armor of God Is God's Son

When we pray, "And do not bring us into temptation, but deliver us from the evil one" (Matt. 6:13), we are affirming our participation in Abba's kingdom and our incorporation into Jesus' resounding defeat of the evil one. In a very real sense, the armor of God is a portrait of Messiah Jesus.

King Jesus is the truth (John 14:6), our righteousness (2 Cor. 5:21), and peace (Eph. 2:14). It is the covenantal faithfulness of Jesus that makes our faith even possible. He is our salvation (Luke 2:30). He is the Word of God (John 1:1, 14). These truths are why the apostle Paul instructs us to "put on the Lord Jesus Christ, and make no provision for the flesh to gratify its desires" (Rom. 13:14).

Prayer as a Way of Life

In God's family, prayer is a way of life. Even Jesus is praying for us right now (Rom. 8:34).

Prayer is the posture of our souls.

Prayer is 24/7 union and communion with the Abba, Son, Spirit.

Prayer reminds us that we are participants of Abba's kingdom, living from Jesus' glory, and becoming transformed into a reflection of Jesus by the Spirit's presence.

> Pray at all times in the Spirit with every prayer
> and request, and stay alert with all perseverance
> and intercession for all the saints. (Eph. 6:18)

———————— Marinate on This ————————

Prayer

Abba,

Messiah Jesus has destroyed the works of the devil.

The cross of Christ disarmed and defeated him.

The resurrection of Christ armed me with power.

In Jesus, by the Spirit's power, I stand in
the strength of resurrection power.

Lord Jesus,

You are my armor. Daily I choose to put you on.

You are the belt of truth, you are my breastplate of
righteousness, your blood is the peace that unifies
me with you and empowers me to rely on you.

You are the faithful one who gives me faith. You
are my salvation. You are the Word of God.

Holy Spirit,

Give me the power to live what I know to be true.

I am more than a conqueror in Christ
who loves me and prays for me.

Amen.

Questions for Reflection

1. Which of the three kinds of temptations resonated with you most? Is there one kind you struggle with most often?

2. Go back and read Ephesians 6:10–18. Which part of the armor of God stands out to you most?

3. What does Pastor Derwin mean by saying that in a very real sense, Jesus *is* the armor of God?

4. What does it mean to "put on Christ"? What changes might God be calling you to make in your life to do this?

Things to Remember

1. Dark powers desire to isolate and separate us from the herd, our brothers and sisters in Christ. In Christ, we protect and strengthen each other.

2. Jesus rewrites the story of Israel from one of disobedience, to one of obedience. Jesus overcomes the temptations of the dark one. By incorporation into his life and story, we are empowered by him to do the same.

3. When we pray, "do not bring us into temptation, but deliver us from the evil one" (Matt. 6:13), we are affirming Jesus' victory. In Christ, we are not helpless. He even gives us battle armor for the war.

4. It is not about the size of your faith; it is about the size of the God your faith is in. Your faith is not primary. Jesus' faithfulness is.

CHAPTER 16

Inhabiting Prayer

 The Lord's Prayer is a gift from Abba.

Like a father on Christmas Day, Abba loves to see his children wake up early, run to the Christmas tree, and unwrap gifts. Abba delights in giving good gifts to his kids (Eph. 1:6).

We do not deserve the gifts, but he is gracious to the undeserving.

He gives grace to unworthy recipients, making us worthy.

His grace is unrivaled.

Abba's greatest gift was not a present under a tree, but Christ's presence nailed to a tree. This gift of grace in Messiah Jesus grants us eternal, unhindered access to our Father.

ABBA'S GREATEST GIFT WAS NOT A PRESENT UNDER A TREE, BUT CHRIST'S PRESENCE NAILED TO A TREE.

> He brought this Good News of peace to you Gentiles who were far away from him, and peace to the Jews who were near. Now all of us can come to the Father through the same Holy Spirit because of what Christ has done for us. (Eph. 2:17–18 NLT)

Abba has provided us 24/7 access to his merciful heart, his glorious kingdom, and his beautiful redemptive purpose for our lives. Abba's heart is that all that went wrong will be made right in Christ. Through his Son, he graciously creates more sons and daughters who join Jesus in righting all the wrongs as they are sculpted into his image.

> God has now revealed to us his mysterious will regarding Christ—which is to fulfill his own good plan. And this is the plan: At the right time he will bring everything together under the authority of Christ—everything in heaven and on earth. (Eph. 1:9–10 NLT)

In the Messiah, we become God's coworkers as the Holy Spirit works to form Christ in us. We become the way Jesus' kingdom is expressed on earth. Until he returns to usher in the new heavens and new earth, we are empowered by his very presence to be salt and light: "In the same way, let your good deeds shine out for all to see, so that everyone will praise your heavenly Father" (Matt. 5:16 NLT).

Abba longs for us to be in communion with him and to have our hearts tuned to his kingdom agenda. Our sacred task is to be his multiethnic family of royal priests. Prayer moves us deeper into understanding and participating in his kingdom. We are contributors to a kingdom that will prevail because the one that was nailed to the cross shed his blood. There is power, unimaginable power, in the blood of the Messiah.

> For God in all his fullness
> was pleased to live in Christ,
> and through him God reconciled
> everything to himself.

He made peace with everything in heaven and
　　on earth
by means of Christ's blood on the cross.
(Col. 1:19–20 NLT)

The Prayer God Always Answers

The Lord's Prayer is the prayer that Abba always answers. We had best believe he is answering our prayers in ways that we may not be able to see now. In the future, we will look back and see his fingerprints of grace. We move forward in life by glancing back at Abba's faithfulness in our lives and remember what he has done.

**THE LORD'S PRAYER IS THE PRAYER
THAT ABBA ALWAYS ANSWERS.**

God does not always do what we want him to do. Our Father does what he wants to do in us and for us, because he is good and working all things to "bring everything together under the authority of Christ—everything in heaven and on earth" (Eph. 1:10 NLT). This is good, because Abba is infinitely wiser than us. He knows what we need better than we do. And he is infinitely more loving than us. He actually wants our good more than we do!

> Work hard to show the results of your salvation, obeying God with deep reverence and fear. For God is working in you, giving you the desire and the power to do what pleases him. (Phil. 2:12–13 NLT)

The Lord's Prayer is a prayer that summons us to abandon our agendas in favor of God's. It enrolls us in the school of Jesus and immerses us in who he is, what he accomplished, and what he wants to accomplish in our lives and creation.

Jesus is the long-awaited Jewish Messiah, the Savior of the world, the eternal Son of God, the Redeemer, the King of kings. He was victorious over sin, death, and evil. By grace through faith, he freed humanity and creation from death and decay (Rom. 8:14–39).

Jesus, by the Spirit's power, now inhabits us to propel us into our divine destinies as royal priests. We now stand at the dangerous intersection of heaven and earth, partners with Jesus and his bride as his kingdom comes to earth.

The Lord's Prayer is big and bold. It is so much bigger and better than just asking for stuff. It is an invitation to participate in the kingdom of God, for the glory of God. This prayer enables us to discover our purpose and passion in God's kingdom.

"Therefore you should pray like this:
Our Father in heaven
your name be honored as holy.
Your kingdom come.
Your will be done on earth
as it is in heaven. Give us today our daily bread.
And forgive us our debts,
as we also have forgiven our debtors.
And do not bring us into temptation,
but deliver us from the evil one."
(Matt. 6:9–13)

The Lord's Prayer is the story of Jesus, and when we pray it, his story becomes our story. Here are ways that I have learned to inhabit a life of prayer.

Praying with One Voice

> As a deer longs for flowing streams, so I long for you, God. (Ps. 42:1)

A life that inhabits prayer is one that longs for Jesus. A life that inhabits prayer is one that recognizes prayer as oxygen to our lungs. A life that inhabits prayer is one that wants Abba for Abba's sake. A life that inhabits prayer is one that thirsts for God, the living God (Ps. 42:2).

One of the ways that my wife, Vicki, inhabits a life of prayer is by practicing the rhythm of grace that we call "praying in one voice." It is a form of corporate prayer.

A few years back, our staff culture at Transformation Church was out of sorts. The spiritual warfare was heavy. The Spirit was doing so much in and through us individually and corporately, but we were struggling to be unified.

We are strongest when we are on our knees in worship and praying to the King. Vicki taught us as a staff to pray with one voice. We would gather in groups of six, but you could do any number. Then we would pray short prayers about the nature and character of Abba based on the Lord's Prayer. Starting with "Our Father in heaven, your name be honored as holy," the prayer looked like this:

Person 1: "Abba, thank you for being good."

Person 2: "Father, thank you for being sovereign."

Person 3: "Father, thank you for never leaving us or forsaking us."

Person 4: "Father, thank you for being all-knowing and all-powerful."

Person 5: "Father, thank you for loving us with an endless, life-giving, sin-killing love."

Person 6: "Father, thank you for your grace."

Then we would sit in silence.

Don't be afraid of the silence. God the Holy Spirit reminds us of the truth of Scripture in this silence.

Then we move to, "Your kingdom come. Your will be done on earth as it is in heaven."

For example:

Person 1: "Abba, thank you that your kingdom has come to earth as it is in heaven."

Person 2: "Lord Jesus, you are the king of the kingdom, we exalt you."

Person 3: "Abba, thank you that we are in your kingdom of light, deliver us from darkness."

Person 4: "Holy Spirit, grant us grace to live out our royal priesthood calling in the kingdom."

Person 5: "Abba, your kingdom is one of joy, love, and truth."

Person 6: "Messiah, we long for your return, but until you do, live your kingdom through us."

Then we sit and soak in silence.
Next, we move to "Give us today our daily bread."

Person 1: "Messiah Jesus, you are the bread of life, who supplies our every need."

Person 2: "King Jesus, meet all my needs, not greeds. Thank you."

Person 3: "Jesus, just as you fed the 5,000, you will daily feed me with your life."

Person 4: "Jesus, you meet my physical needs, so we bless others in your name."

Person 5: "Jesus, you are my provider and sustainer."

Person 6: "Messiah, I will seek Abba's kingdom and righteousness and not worry about my needs."

We marinate in the moment, soaking in his presence.

Then we move to "And forgive us our debts, as we also have forgiven our debtors."

> **Person 1:** "Jesus, thank you for being the Lamb of God who takes away the sins of the world."

> **Person 2:** "Messiah, thank you for purifying and cleansing us from our sins."

> **Person 3:** "Jesus, thank you for casting our sins into the sea of Abba's forgotten memory."

> **Person 4:** "Jesus, your blood is our peace and reconciliation with Abba and each other."

> **Person 5:** "Holy Spirit, give me the grace to forgive those who hurt me."

> **Person 6:** "Jesus, we are forgiven to become forgivers."

Silence. Then we transition to "And do not bring us into temptation, but deliver us from the evil one."

> **Person 1:** "Abba, we stand in King Jesus' victory over sin, death, and the evil one. Thank you."

> **Person 2:** "Lord Jesus, by the Spirit's power, you are the armor of God."

Person 3: "Holy Spirit, bless us so we can see that our enemy is not people, but the dark powers."

Person 4: "Abba, you fight our battles, the victory is won through the blood of the Lamb."

Person 5: "Jesus, it is our joy to put you on so we will not fulfill the desires of the flesh."

Person 6: "King Jesus, you have made us weapons of righteousness to slay the darkness."

Once again, do not be afraid of the silence.

Sit and soak. Marinate.

Attune your heart to the Messiah through the Spirit. Enjoy the oneness with God and your brothers and sisters in Christ. Praying in one voice not only transformed our staff, but it has also transformed our church. Our worship, praise, unity, discipleship, and hunger to reach the lost has blossomed.

Marriages are being reconciled.

Addiction is being defeated.

The hungry are being fed.

Justice is being implemented.

Prayer is the cyclonic wind of grace that blows on the sails of the church, moving her into her destiny of bringing heaven to earth.

PRAYER IS THE CYCLONIC WIND OF GRACE THAT BLOWS ON THE SAILS OF THE CHURCH, MOVING HER INTO HER DESTINY OF BRINGING HEAVEN TO EARTH.

Praying Scripture

Another practice that can boost the power of our prayer lives is praying the God-breathed Scriptures directly. I learned how to pray the Scriptures as the Spirit of God was moving to address trauma in my life. Entering God's kingdom is instantaneous. Growing as a citizen of God's kingdom takes a lifetime. This is called progressive sanctification. Praying Scripture is healing my hurts. Throughout the day, I will pray the following verses:

> LORD my God, I cried to you for help, and you healed me. (Ps. 30:2)

> He himself bore our sins in his body on the tree; so that, having died to sins, we might live for righteousness. By his wounds, you have been healed. (1 Pet. 2:24)

> He heals the brokenhearted and bandages their wounds. He counts the number of the stars; he gives names to all of them. Our Lord is great, vast in power; his understanding is infinite. (Ps. 147:3–5)

Bask in Scripture.
Sit in it.
Eat the Bible.

> All Scripture is inspired by God, and is profitable for teaching, for rebuking, for correcting, for training in righteousness, so that the man of God may be complete, equipped for every good work. (2 Tim. 3:16–17)

Ken Boa's books, *Face to Face: Praying the Scriptures, Volume One* and *Volume Two*, have been super helpful in teaching me how to pray the Scriptures for myself, but also as a means of praying for others.

I also use an ancient spiritual practice called *lectio divina*, or sacred reading. First, prayerfully select a short passage of Scripture and read over it several times. Second, marinate on it for a few minutes. Ask questions of the text. Let the Holy Spirit examine your heart and reveal God's heart through the texts. Third, in response to the text, write a prayer to Abba. Fourth, contemplate your prayer and the Scripture in silence. Just be with God.

Scripture informs and transforms our prayer lives. The more familiar we are with Scripture, the more familiar we will be with Jesus and his redemptive purposes.

SCRIPTURE INFORMS AND TRANSFORMS OUR PRAYER LIVES.

> He said to them, "How foolish you are, and how slow to believe all that the prophets have spoken! Wasn't it necessary for the Messiah to suffer these things and enter into his glory?" Then beginning with Moses and all the Prophets, he interpreted for them the things concerning himself in all the Scriptures. (Luke 24:25–27)

The Bible is not about us. But it is for us. Read the Bible Christo-centrically (with Christ at the center; John 5:39–40). All Scripture is a gift to you so you will know Jesus and *enter* into him and his purposes for your lives. In him, we are royal priests, ambassadors, and ministers of reconciliation, representing the King of the kingdom (2 Cor. 5:18–21).

We can also pray the Psalms. The Psalms are songs and prayers that have guided, comforted, and inspired Abba's people for several thousand years. The elements of the Lord's Prayer fill the Psalms. Use them as a guide.

Just about every night, I pray from memory Psalm 23. This passage reminds me of who Abba is and what he accomplished in Jesus on my behalf. I go to sleep with the Word of God on my mind, and I wake up with the Word of God on my mind. Scripture-informed prayer sets our minds on things above where Christ is seated (Col. 3:1–3) and where we are seated with him (Eph. 2:6).

Prayer Is a Posture of the Soul

We inhabit prayer when it becomes a posture of our souls. To "pray constantly" as Paul encourages us to do (1 Thess. 5:17) means to have a heart anchored in Jesus, giving us a holy awareness to his presence through the Holy Spirit. To inhabit a life of prayer is to abide in him and to walk in the Spirit (John 15:5; Gal. 5:22–24). We are to live intentionally with a Godward gaze.

As you grow in prayer, you will develop your own unique rhythms. There have been times that I write out morning, noon, and night prayers. Other periods I have spent a week just praying and marinating on the character of God.

Through the structure of The Lord's Prayer, we will intercede on behalf of others. The Lord's Prayer is designed to be communal, not merely individualistic. There is only "us" in the Lord's Prayer. Interceding on behalf of people deepens our unity with our brothers and sisters. Unity creates a greater and more beautiful community. Jesus' prayer is that we would be one because of our unity and love for each other, showing the world that Jesus came from Abba to rescue and reconcile the world through his precious blood.

> "May they also be in us, so that the world may believe you sent me. I have given them the glory you have given me, so that they may be one as we are one. I am in them and you are in me, so that they may be made completely one, that the world may know you have sent me and have loved them as you have loved me." (John 17:21–23)

Should We Pray for Healing?

Gary was a good brother. He had a big personality to go along with his 6'6" frame, and he loved Jesus. Sadly, Gary was diagnosed with stomach cancer. After his surgery, I went to the hospital and read Scripture to him while he was sleeping. As I read, I heard him mumbling sounds. The more I read, the more I recognized that he was speaking the Scripture back to me. He would wake up quoting Scripture. This experience blessed my soul.

The last time I saw Gary, his 6'6", 270-pound body was down to under 100 pounds. He had been unconscious for several days. I sat down next to his bed and started reading Scripture. After a few minutes, I heard Gary mumble. The more I read Scripture, the more he mumbled. He became louder and even started lifting his arms to praise.

Cancer could steal Gary's body, but it could not steal his praise.

Gary knew that to be absent from the body is to be present with King Jesus (2 Cor. 5:8).

Gary knew that his healing was guaranteed in the resurrection.

Gary died, but he lived again instantly. He was healed. In the future, his soul will be reunited with his body. He will have a glorified, resurrected body in the new heavens and new earth (1 Cor. 15:53–58).

Should we pray for healing when people are sick? Yes, we should. This is important to discuss here, because you may get the idea from my encouragement to pray the Lord's Prayer, and to trust that God knows what we need, that we shouldn't ask him for things like healing. But of course we should! He is our Father!

For those in Christ, healing is guaranteed—it is called the resurrection. There are times that Abba will physically heal us of sickness here on earth, but even those who are healed will eventually die. Our ultimate healing is the resurrection. Do not ever let anyone guilt you by saying that if you have more faith you would be healed! At the same time, don't let anyone guilt you and make you feel unspiritual for asking for healing now!

In Jesus' day, the sick were considered unclean; therefore, they were forbidden to enter the temple. When Jesus healed them, he told them to go show the priest they were no longer unclean. When Jesus came, the Messiah healed the sick. Now that Jesus has ascended to glory, the sign that the Messiah came is resurrection.

Early in my ministry, I went to the hospital and prayed for a little girl with fiery red hair. Her vital organs were shutting down, but the doctors had no clue as to why. She was hooked up to all kinds of machines. Before I prayed, I sensed a prompting to ask the child's father to place his hands on her head. I placed my hands on him. I cannot remember what I prayed, but I remember what happened. The next day, the dad called me and said his daughter was in perfect health and the doctors had no explanation.

I believe the Lord used my prayers and so many other prayers to heal the little girl with red hair. Eventually, like the rest of us, she will die. Then, because she is in Christ, she will experience ultimate healing in the resurrection.

Should we pray for healing? Yes, because Abba has guaranteed our ultimate healing. Because Jesus rose from the dead, so shall we.

The Prayers of Paul

The apostle Paul also inhabited a life of prayer. Paul was intoxicated by the person and work of Jesus. Jesus profoundly shaped the prayer life of the apostle Paul. Like Jesus, Paul's prayers are soaked with Old Testament Scripture. Paul's prayers were Jesus-centric, kingdom of God shaped, and gospel-focused. Here are a few examples of Paul's prayers that highlight themes of the Lord's Prayer, such as Abba's greatness, his love in Messiah, the kingdom of God, Abba's provision, the atonement, and our victory in Christ over sin, death, and evil.

> I never stop giving thanks for you as I remember you in my prayers. I pray that the God of our Lord Jesus Christ, the glorious Father, would give you the Spirit of wisdom and revelation in the knowledge of him. I pray that the eyes of your heart may be enlightened so that you may know what is the hope of his calling, what is the wealth of his glorious inheritance in the saints, and what is the immeasurable greatness of his power toward us

who believe, according to the mighty working of his strength. He exercised this power in Christ by raising him from the dead and seating him at his right hand in the heavens—far above every ruler and authority, power and dominion, and every title given, not only in this age but also in the one to come. And he subjected everything under his feet, and appointed him as head over everything for the church, which is his body, the fullness of the one who fills all things in every way. (Eph. 1:16–23)

Don't worry about anything, but in everything, through prayer and petition with thanksgiving, present your requests to God. And the peace of God, which surpasses all understanding, will guard your hearts and minds in Christ Jesus. (Phil. 4:6–7)

May our Lord Jesus Christ himself and God our Father, who has loved us and given us eternal encouragement and good hope by grace, encourage your hearts and strengthen you in every good work and word. In addition, brothers and sisters, pray for us that the word of the Lord may spread rapidly and be honored, just as it was with you, and that we may be delivered from wicked and evil people, for not all have faith. But the Lord is faithful; he will strengthen you and guard you from the evil one. We have confidence in the Lord about you, that you are doing and will continue to do what we command. May the Lord direct your hearts to God's love and Christ's endurance. (2 Thess. 2:16–3:5)

Now may the God who gives endurance and encouragement grant you to live in harmony with one another, according to Christ Jesus, so that you may glorify the God and Father of our Lord Jesus Christ with one mind and one voice. (Rom. 15:5–6)

My Prayer for You

Thank you for taking this journey through the Lord's Prayer with me. My prayer is that your love for Abba, the Son, and Spirit has grown and is making your life beautiful. I pray that your role as a royal priest in the kingdom of God has inspired you to walk in your calling to make much of Jesus by displaying his kingdom on earth as it is in heaven. I pray that you know that Jesus will meet all your needs and that generosity will be the aroma of your life. I pray that the forgiveness you have freely received will be generously given away to those who have hurt you. I pray that every single day you would put on the armor of God and light up the darkness.

This may be the end of the book, but I pray it is not the end of our friendship. I pray you would revisit these pages often, over the years, and that you would use this book to journey with others as they unwrap the gift of the Lord's Prayer.

I join with the apostle Paul in praying this over you and your loved ones:

When I think of all this, I fall to my knees and pray to the Father, the Creator of everything in heaven and on earth. I pray that from his glorious, unlimited resources he will empower you with inner strength through his Spirit. Then Christ will make his home in your hearts as you trust in him. Your roots will grow down into God's love and keep you strong. And may you have the power to understand, as all God's people should, how wide, how long, how high, and how deep his love is. May you experience the love of Christ, though it is too great to understand fully. Then you will be made complete with all the fullness of life and power that comes from God. Now all glory to God, who is able, through his mighty power at work within us, to accomplish infinitely more than we might ask or think. Glory to him in the church and in Christ Jesus through all generations forever and ever! Amen. (Eph. 3:14–21 NLT)

Your brother,
Derwin

Questions for Reflection

1. As you have been reading this book, how has your prayer life changed so far?

2. What is your experience in praying for healing? How does the confidence we have in the resurrection change our understanding of praying for healing?

3. What is the one thing in this book that has most stood out to you and stuck with you?

4. What actions do you plan to take moving forward to move into a life of inhabiting prayer?

Things to Remember

1. The Lord's Prayer is a prayer that summons us to abandon our agendas in favor of God's. It enrolls us in the school of Jesus and immerses us in who he is, what he accomplished, and what he wants to accomplish in our lives and creation.

2. The Lord's Prayer is big and bold. It is so much bigger and better than just asking for stuff. It is an invitation to participate in the kingdom of God, for the glory of God.

3. Scripture informs and transforms our prayer lives. The more familiar we are with Scripture, the more familiar we will be with Jesus and his redemptive purposes.

4. Paul's prayers were Jesus-centric, kingdom of God shaped, and gospel-focused.

ALSO AVAILABLE
FROM DERWIN L. GRAY

Everyone wants to be happy. We spend our money, time, and energy chasing after "the good life," and we run ourselves into physical, mental, and emotional exhaustion on the way. But what if the happiness we're all striving for isn't the happiness we were created for?

Discover the good life you were meant for through Jesus' teaching in the Beatitudes.

AVAILABLE WHEREVER BOOKS ARE SOLD

CHRISTIAN
STANDARD
BIBLE®

"

"I preach and teach from the Christian Standard Bible because of the accuracy, precision, and beauty of the text. I'm excited to finally have one translation that is both faithful to the authorial intent of the biblical writers and written in English that communicates to this generation."

DR. DERWIN L. GRAY

Accurate. Readable. Shareable. **Learn more at CSBible.com**

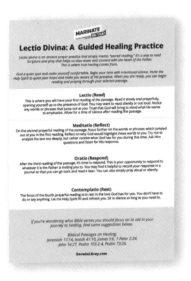